D1495716

THE STORY OF
AMERICA'S
RAILROADS

· CONNECTING · A · CONTINENT ·

THE STORY OF AMERICA'S
RAILROADS

**Ray Spangenburg
and Diane K. Moser**

Facts On File
New York • Oxford

To all the railroad people—
engineers, track layers, conductors,
entrepreneurs and hobos—
and to all who love the haunting sound
of faraway train whistles and clacking wheels

The Story of America's Railroads
Copyright © 1991 by Ray Spangenburg and Diane K. Moser

Facts On File, Inc.
460 Park Avenue South
New York NY 10016
USA

Facts On File Limited
Collins Street
Oxford OX4 1XJ
United Kingdom

Library of Congress Cataloging-in-Publication Data

Spangenburg, Ray, 1939–
The story of America's railroads / by Ray Spangenburg and Diane K. Moser.
p. cm. — (Connecting a continent)
Includes bibliographical references and index.
Summary: Traces the history of railroads in America, focusing on the technology, people,
and life on the railroads.
ISBN 0-8160-2257-7
1. Railroads—United States—History—Juvenile literature.
[1. Railroads—History.] I. Moser, Diane, 1944– . II. Title.
III. Series: Spangenburg, Ray, 1939– Connecting a continent.
TF23.S72 1991   91-11553

British CIP data available on request from Facts On File.

Text and Jacket design by Donna Sinisgalli
Composition by Facts On File, Inc.
Manufactured by the Maple-Vail Book Manufacturing Group
Printed in the United States of America

10 9 8 7 6 5 4 3 2 1

This book is printed on acid-free paper.

CONTENTS

ACKNOWLEDGMENTS

We'd like to thank the many individuals, too numerous to name, who helped us on this project—we greatly appreciated both their aid and enthusiasm. Several made special contributions, going out of their way to help make this book better, including, especially, Anne Bennof of the Association of American Railroads, as well as: Anne Calhoun of the B&O Museum; Bob Durham; Dave Letourneau of the Burlington Northern Railroad; Connie Menninger, manuscripts archivist at the Kansas State Historical Society; and Bill Shank of the American Canal and Transportation Center. A special thanks also to our editor at Facts On File, James Warren, for his many insightful suggestions in shaping this series.

1

BIRTH OF THE IRON HORSE

The story of railroads begins, in a way, far back in human history with three inventions: the wheel (in Sumeria, some 5,000 years ago), the first use of iron to fashion objects in about 1500 B.C. and the first use of steam as a source of power—because all of these inventions contributed to the birth of the beast known as "the iron horse," the steam locomotive.

Tracks, another key ingredient for the birth of the railroad, came into use as early as the first few centuries A.D. when the Romans built rails of cut stone. By laying rails through areas plagued by mud and muck, they discovered their wagons could avoid the mire. As a result, combinations of track and flanged wheels came into use all over Europe. By 1630 U-shaped tracks were used at Newcastle, England—although the vehicles that ran on them were still drawn by horses.

Meanwhile, in the early 1700s, a blacksmith at Dartmouth, England, Thomas Newcomen, and his partner, Thomas Savery, built one of the first steam-powered engines—they called it a "fire engine"—to pump water. They applied for a patent in 1705, and theirs and similar engines soon came into widespread use in the coal processing plants of northern England.

The first inventor credited with use of a steam engine to move a vehicle, however, was French. In 1769 Nicolas Cugnot devised a strange-looking three-wheeled vehicle to tow cannons. With its kettle-shaped engine mounted on the front, Cugnot's invention made its debut at a snail's pace of two to three miles an hour and had to stop every 10 or 15 minutes to build up a new fire in the boiler. When Cugnot staged a demonstration of his new machine, it plowed into a wall. He had forgotten

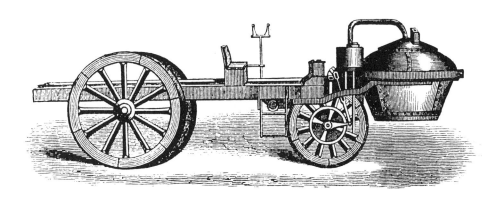

Cugnot's engine. Samuel Smiles, *The Life of George Stephenson and of his son Robert Stephenson,* 1868

A typical English colliery similar to those where George Stephenson worked. Smiles, *The Life of George Stephenson*, 1868

an important component: the brakes. Still, it was the first road vehicle ever powered by steam instead of a horse.

Across the ocean, at least one futurist in America also saw the possibilities of steam power in this period before the American Revolution in 1776. Regarded by his countrymen as a wild-eyed eccentric, Philadelphia blacksmith Oliver Evans proposed a sort of steam-propelled carriage riding on a system of rails to run between Philadelphia and New York. He said:

> The time will come when carriages propelled by steam will be in general use, traveling at the rate of fifteen to twenty miles an hour, or 300 miles a day, as fast as birds can fly, passing through the air with such velocity as to be a most exhilarating exercise. To accomplish this two sets of railways will be laid, so nearly level as not to deviate more than 2° from horizontal, made of wood or iron, on a smooth path of broken stone or gravel to guide the carriages so they may pass each other in opposite directions as they will travel by night as well as by day. Passengers will sleep in these stages as comfortably as they do now at stage coach inns.

Furthermore, Evans went on,

> Twenty miles per hour is about thirty-two feet a second and the resistance of the air about one pound a square foot; but the body of the carriages will be shaped like a swift swimming fish to pass easily through the air. The United States will be the first nation to make the discovery, and her wealth and power will rise to unparalleled heights.

Unfortunately, no one took Evans seriously at the time.

Back in the British Isles, however, the Industrial Revolution was moving into full swing. It was a time that saw the birth of large-scale production as machines and power tools began to replace hand tools in industry after industry, a time of fast-moving, even sometimes frightening, economic and social change.

In the late 18th century, Scottish inventor James Watt was asked to repair a steam engine. Watt, always stretching his mind in search of new possibilities, rebuilt it instead, adding a rotary motion. Now he had an engine that could be used for locomotion. This set the stage for his assistant from Cornwall, England, William Murdock, who built a small steam-powered car in 1784. Late one night in Redruth, Cornwall, Murdock decided to test the car—but, much to his surprise, the reckless buggy sped off without him. As it snorted and puffed wildly through the dark cobblestone streets, the story goes, the local vicar encountered the speeding monster and swore later he'd seen the devil himself.

Murdock never did much more with the idea, but his experiment inspired Richard Trevithick, also of Cornwall, who built several steam-propelled carriages and in 1804 he tested the first "true railway locomotive." In a demonstration Trevithick's engine pulled five wagons carrying an impressive 10-ton load and 70 passengers. The train moved at about five miles an hour over a cast-iron tramway that served an ironworks in South Wales. Unfortunately, the demonstration destroyed the track, which was too fragile for the heavy load, but the test was a success.

Not until June of 1812, however, did the first regularly working railway locomotive go into service. Its inventors were John Blenkinsop and Matthew Murray of Leeds, England. They needed a way to haul coal without using horses, because feed for horses had

become too expensive due to the Napoleonic Wars. The result was the Blenkinsop/Murray locomotive, which used four nondriving wheels to carry the weight while a cogged drive wheel pulled it along a cogged track.

Within a few years they had several locomotives running, and Blenkinsop/Murray locomotives continued in use until the 1830s.

But the real father of the railway was born June 9, 1781, in the little northern English coal-mining village of Wylam, just west of Newcastle-upon-Tyne. One of six children, George Stephenson grew up working in and around the mines. Though he never learned to read (there was no time for schooling), he quickly demonstrated an aptitude for machines, particularly steam-powered machines.

By 1814 Stephenson had designed his first "travelling engine," which he named Blucher. He incorporated some features of the Blenkinsop/Murray

The Stephenson's Rocket locomotive. Smiles, *The Life of George Stephenson,* 1868

Technology Close-Up

THE STEAM LOCOMOTIVE AND HOW IT WORKS

As everyone who has boiled a kettle of water knows, steam is produced by heating water above 212 degrees Fahrenheit. But the volume of steam produced is 1,700 times greater than the water that produced it—so when it's confined, steam produces pressure. By making use of this principle, a steam engine can translate steam pressure to power—locomotive power.

Basically a steam locomotive's engine has two parts—the boiler and the engine itself. The boiler is a closed container usually with a firebox located at the rear. Steam produced in the boiler passes through a valve (the regulator or throttle) into the engine cylinder. There it expands, forcing the piston to move, which in turn transmits motion to the driving wheels via a connecting rod. When the steam is spent, it passes out through a blast pipe, into the smokebox and up the chimney.

The engine requires a supply of both water and fuel, usually wood or coal, to run. Some locomotives carry water and fuel supplies on a separate car, or tender, in which case they are known as tender locomotives. A tank locomotive, on the other hand, carries one or more water tanks on the locomotive itself.

---

design—the Blucher's boiler was a similar horizontal eight-foot cylinder with a diameter of about three feet, and he ran a tube through the boiler to carry hot gases from the fire. But he used smooth wheels and relied on friction, particularly because he designed the engine for the Killingworth Colliery, where the tracks were smooth and L-shaped to fit a groove in the wheels. The Blucher first operated on July 25, 1814. Over the next few years Stephenson continued to develop other small coal-hauling engines.

Almost by accident, the first plan to build a railroad transportation system in England was established in 1821 when the British Parliament awarded a charter to the county of Durham to build a sort of public tramway. The route would run from the port of Stockton near the North Sea (on the River Tees) 12 miles to the coal fields at Darlington. When George Stephenson suggest the use of steam locomotives to Edward Pease, the promoter, Pease had thought horses would do. But Stephenson contended that a Stephenson locomotive could do the work of 50 horses. As Pease later recalled, "There was such an honest, sensible look about him, and he seemed so modest and unpretending." The line hired Stephenson as chief engineer, who engaged his son, Robert, to help survey the line.

Born in 1803, Robert Stephenson, unlike his father, was well educated—first at Newcastle and then at the University of Edinburgh, where he won a prize in mathematics. When he returned home, he read all his notes on science and mathematics aloud to his delighted father, who had never learned to read or write well. The father-and-son team they soon formed combined the father's shrewdness and ingenuity with the son's intelligence and formal learning.

With Pease's help, the Stephensons established their factory at Newcastle in 1823. The first engine the new company completed was an eight-ton locomotive called the Locomotion, which was designed to haul coal. George Stephenson convinced the directors to build rails of iron, not wood—and not cast iron, which he had seen break easily at Killingworth, but malleable iron from Sweden. He also established the standard of 4 feet 8½ inches as the width between rails, a standard that, though much-disputed at various times, still holds to this day.

The Stockton & Darlington Rail-Way opened September 27, 1825. The train consisted of the Locomotion, its tender, six cars of coal and flour bags, a boxlike passenger coach that carried the directors (the first passenger car in history), 21 open freight cars with benches and six more coal cars.

Hundreds of excited onlookers piled on. The train made the 12-mile trip at an average of eight miles an hour, carrying a load estimated at nearly 90 tons—compared to the horse-drawn Surrey Iron Railway, which took two hours to pull a 55-ton load a distance of six miles. The canal and turnpike operators, who had turned out hoping to see a fiery disaster and an end to the upstart railroad, left bitterly disappointed.

The Stockton & Darlington continued to use horses instead of steam much of the time, but the Stephensons went on to campaign for the building of a steam-operated railroad between Liverpool and Manchester. They faced heavy opposition from the turnpike companies competing for the same traffic and the Duke of Bridgewater's canal company (which had a monopoly on hauling freight) as well as many of the country gentry who were still not happy with the innovations of the Industrial Revolution. Five years later, however, the Stephensons succeeded in obtaining a charter from Parliament and began building the steam-powered Liverpool and Manchester Railway.

By this time, Robert Stephenson, now in his twenties, ran the factory himself, and in October 1829 his engine called Rocket won the trials at Rainhill against two other steam engines. His victory was dampened, however, when in all the confusion William Huskisson, a member of Parliament for Liverpool, fell in front of the Rocket. After loading the severely injured Huskisson onto another locomotive, George Stephenson raced to the nearest hospital, hitting speeds of 36 miles per hour. Huskisson died, unfortunately, but even this accident didn't cast a pall on England's growing enthusiasm for the steam locomotive.

Not many months later George Stephenson had a more pleasant experience when he gave a ride to Fanny Kemble, a beautiful young actress, on the Northumbrian, another locomotive built by Robert. She later wrote somewhat colorfully that "The engine was set off at its utmost speed, 35 miles an hour, swifter than a bird flies. You cannot conceive what that sensation of cutting air was; the motion as smooth as possible, too. I stood up, and with my bonnet off drank the air before me."

For the railroad, the stage was set for an ever-brightening future, a future of possibilities, of speed and success. It was entirely natural that its spirit would next be caught by a rapidly growing country across the Atlantic Ocean.

2

RAILROADS ARRIVE IN AMERICA
1812–1832

In 1812, the same year Blenkinsop and Murray first put a steam locomotive to work in England, a curious publication was making the rounds of the commercial and political community in America. Its title was long, awkward and unenchanting: *Documents Tending to Prove the Superior Advantages of Rail-ways and Steam carriages over Canal Navigation*. Initially, not many people bothered to read the little pamphlet, and the few who did viewed it as the work of a crank.

TRANSPORTATION FOR A GROWING NATION

Although the nation was still young, Americans were just beginning to recognize that their country needed better transportation. So far, since the founding of the colonies along the Atlantic Ocean in the 17th century, Americans had managed to get around reasonably well by using natural waterways and a few overland roads. But, following the revolution in 1776, the population had both grown steadily and spread out from the coastal communities. In 1803 the Louisiana Purchase added more than a million square miles of new territory and doubled the nation's land area.

Exploration of the Louisiana Territory by Meriwether Lewis and William Clark established the attractiveness of the new lands, and westward expansion was very much a reality. Overland transportation

became an obvious necessity for economic growth, with supply lines and trade routes urgently needed to provide connections between the harbors of coastal cities and the coal fields, farmlands and trappers to the west.

In response to these needs, a few areas had begun to develop better roads (the Philadelphia-Lancaster Turnpike, 61 miles of hard-surfaced toll road, completed in 1794; the Natchez Road, to stretch 500 miles from Nashville, Tennessee to Natchez, Mississippi, chartered in 1806; the Cumberland Road, to connect Cumberland, Maryland with the town of Wheeling on the Ohio River, begun in 1811). By 1812, 5,000 miles of surfaced roads had spread through the countryside, and there were many more unsurfaced roads.

Many people, though, believed that the nation's future lay in the building of canals, which could carry people and goods faster, cheaper and more efficiently than horseback or wagon. As far back as 1762 a survey had been started for a canal from the Susquehanna River at Middletown to the Schuylkill River at Reading, Pennsylvania. By 1794 a canal eased traffic past South Hadley Falls on the Connecticut River in western Massachusetts. In South Carolina the 22-mile Santee Canal connected the Santee and Cooper rivers by 1800. Plans for other canals sparked interest up and down the coast, including an adventurous project called the Erie Canal, which would stretch over 363

Trains and Dates

EARLY RAILROADS IN AMERICA
1800–1832

1807 A tramway of wooden rails, powered partly by gravity, partly by horse, begins operating in Boston.

1809 Thomas Leiper connects quarries in Delaware County, Pennsylvania with the coast, using a horse-drawn wooden tramway.

1815 The New Jersey Legislature grants the first railroad charter in America to John Stevens. He did not succeed in building his planned railroad between the Delaware and Raritan rivers, however.

1825 John Stevens's locomotive begins operation on a half-mile circular track on his estate in Hoboken, New Jersey. It is the first locomotive to run on rails in the nation.

1826 On October 7 the Granite Railway, opened by Gridley Bryant at Quincy, Massachusetts, begins operation of horse-drawn cars along its three-mile track to transport granite to the site of the Bunker Hill Monument.

1827 February 28. The Baltimore & Ohio Railroad is chartered by the State of Maryland. Construction begins July 4, 1828.

   December 19. South Carolina grants permission to build the South Carolina Canal & Railroad, later part of the Southern Railroad.

1829 August 8. The Stourbridge Lion, a locomotive imported from England, is operated by Horatio Allen along a three-mile stretch of track owned by the Delaware & Hudson. It is the first steam locomotive to run on commercial track in the United States.

   December 21. The B&O completes the first large railroad bridge in the United States, the Carrollton Viaduct, just outside of Baltimore.

1830 January 7. The B&O begins daily runs between Baltimore and Ellicott's Mills, Maryland.

   Lewis Wernwag completes the first timber railroad bridge in the United States.

   The Tom Thumb, built by Peter Cooper, makes a round-trip trial run from Baltimore to Ellicott's Mills. It is the first American-built steam locomotive to run on commercial tracks.

   December 25. The Best Friend of Charleston, an American-built steam locomotive, begins the first scheduled steam passenger service at Charleston, South Carolina.

1831 August 9. The locomotive DeWitt Clinton of the Mohawk and Hudson line hauls the first steam train in New York State, from Albany to Schenectady.

   November 12. Passenger service begins between New York City and Philadelphia. The locomotive John Bull provides the power between Camden and Amboy, New Jersey. Water connections at each end complete the journey.

   November. The South Carolina Canal and Railroad Company provides the first mail service by rail.

1832 The first streetcar (horse-drawn) in the world begins operating in New York City (New York and Harlem Railroad).

miles from Albany to Buffalo, New York. "Canal fever" had set in. These giant ditches with their locks and towpaths appeared to be the exciting wave of the future in 1812, a wave of certain prosperity for any community otherwise isolated from its markets and suppliers. Little wonder that most serious-minded businessmen and politicians scoffed at the idea that the railroad was the mode of transport for the future.

JOHN STEVENS'S DREAM

For the author of *Documents Tending to Prove the Superior Advantages of Rail-ways and Steam carriages over Canal Navigation*, however, the idea was far more than just interesting.

The son of an indentured clerk, as a boy John Stevens had watched persistence pay off as his father worked his way out of poverty to become a successful merchant and politician. Stevens himself attended King's College (now Columbia University) and, armed with a strong education combined with the determination and fortitude he had learned from his father, he developed a passionate belief in the steam engine. In 1789 he petitioned the New York State legislature for exclusive rights to build and operate a steamboat. His petition was denied, but in 1804 he actually built a small steam craft called *Little Juliana*, which although experimental was well ahead of its time. Convinced of the potential of steam, two years later he built a much bigger boat, the *Phoenix*, which he again hoped would win him a monopoly to operate in the New York waters. This time, though, he was outpaced by another visionary, Robert Fulton, whose steamboat *Clermont* proved itself first and won for Fulton the rights that Stevens had tried to obtain.

Nonetheless, Stevens had seen the potential of steam power beyond its uses in stationary engines. By 1810 he had become an outspoken champion of steam locomotives and railway construction.

Actually the idea of a "rail-way," that is, a "road built of rails," was not entirely unknown in the United States. The first primitive "rail-road" was built in Boston in 1807, when a simple gravity-and-cable arrangement was used to move dirt and gravel by way of wooden tracks. It was obvious—whether using manpower, cables, gravity or horses—that it was easier to push or pull a wheeled vehicle over anchored tracks than over rough earth, and the method was often used by other small industries and quarries over short distances.

John Stevens built a small, circular track at his home where he ran a demonstration locomotive. S. C. Williams Library, Stevens Institute of Technology, Hoboken, New Jersey

Peter Cooper's Tom Thumb lost this spirited race against a horse, but the "iron horse" would soon take over the transportation scene.
Association of American Railroads

What was difficult to accept about Stevens's idea was that tracks could be laid for dozens, even hundreds of miles and that the power for moving such a transportation system should be a self-propelling steam engine riding on the tracks. In the early 1800s few people thought the proposition was technically feasible. And those who had invested in canals, roads and wagon companies fought bitterly against the economic threat of Stevens's "crackpot" ideas. Gouverneur Morris of New York State, who was involved heavily in the Erie Canal, flatly announced that a railroad as envisioned by Stevens was impossible "under any circumstance." One canal corporation even enlisted the aid of a prominent scientist to lecture against the idea of a railroad, warning the public that trains, if they could travel as fast as some people believed, would jostle the brains of passengers and cause them permanent damage.

Stevens, it appeared, was fighting a losing battle. Through sheer force of will he did manage to convince the New Jersey legislature in 1815 to grant him a charter to build a railroad, but he couldn't get enough money or credit to back him and was forced to abandon the scheme. A second charter, this one from the Pennsylvania legislature in 1823, also lapsed

before Stevens could scrape together the money to begin building. In the end, to prove that a railroad could actually run, he settled for building and operating a small, cabless steam locomotive on a half-mile circular track on his estate in Hoboken, New Jersey. It was the first steam locomotive to be run on a track in the United States. While it wasn't much more than a toy engine, it ran, and Stevens proudly demonstrated it to anyone who was curious enough to come and take a look.

Like other visionaries, John Stevens was ahead of his time. The irony was that he was actually not that far ahead of it. Less than a dozen years after his small locomotive steamed forlornly around its track in Hoboken, the steam locomotive and railroad began to change American history.

THE STEAM LOCOMOTIVE COMES TO AMERICA

While opposition continued, not everyone in America ignored John Stevens, and not everyone was blind to the possibilities of railroads. News of the progress of railroads in England soon attracted supporters in the United States, and in 1826, at a joint session of Con-

9

Focus on People

PETER COOPER AND THE TOM THUMB

When he told the directors of the pioneer Baltimore and Ohio Railroad that he thought he could "knock together something," Peter Cooper (1791–1883) had no idea he would become famous for building the first American steam locomotive to run on a chartered railroad in the United States.

Cooper's tiny engine, called the Tom Thumb, was built in several iron foundries that he owned and operated. (Coincidentally Cooper, who would help put horse-drawn cargo carriers out of business, had made his fortune by manufacturing glue—made from horses' hooves.)

Although the miniature Tom Thumb managed to generate only about 1.43 horsepower, it made history on August 28, 1830 by pushing an open car carrying 18 passengers along a 14-mile stretch of the Baltimore and Ohio tracks. The trip took about an hour and a quarter. Perhaps flushed by the tiny locomotive's success, the engineer challenged a horse-drawn train to a race on its return trip. According to witnesses, the Tom Thumb was well in the lead when it developed engine trouble and lost the race (much to the excitement of those who opposed the railroads).

Intended only as an experiment, the engine never actually carried passengers again along the B&O's regularly scheduled route.

Cooper, who had many other interests, also made several other contributions to America's growth. His blast furnaces were the first in the country to use the Bessemer process, which revolutionized the use of steel in civil engineering and construction. He later became president of the company that helped finance the first permanent transatlantic cable as well as president of the American Telephone Company. And, having had only one year of formal schooling himself, Cooper also led the fight to establish New York City's first free public school system.

gress, U.S. Senator Oliver H. Smith of Indiana spoke out: "I tell you that in England they have already run railroads full loaded at 30 miles per hour and they will yet be run at higher speeds in America. . . ."

Still unconvinced, one heckler in the audience shouted out, "Either you are crazy, or you think we are fools for a man could not live at that speed!" The detractor expressed an opinion shared by many well-educated people, but such fears would not stand for long in the way of the growing need for faster, more efficient transport.

Even while Stevens was laying the track for his tiny locomotive, a small group of civic-minded Philadelphians was thinking over what he had to say. The group, calling itself The Pennsylvania Society for the Promotion of Internal Improvements, saw that although Philadelphia was then the largest city in the country and had the busiest seaport, both the city and state now faced losing much of that economic edge. When the Erie Canal was completed in 1825, much of Philadelphia's commerce would shift to New York City, which also had an excellent harbor and would

now also have cheap, direct transportation connections across the state to the Great Lakes. The Pennsylvania group decided to send engineer William Strickland to England to study how canals and railroads might be used to solve their problems. Strickland was impressed by what he saw. When he returned, he recommended that the State of Pennsylvania build both—railroads over hilly stretches and canals through the flatlands—to solve its growing transportation problems.

Some other engineers had also begun to think along the same lines. Among them was John Jervis, chief engineer for the Delaware and Hudson Canal Company, which owned and operated a profitable group of coal mines at Carbondale, Pennsylvania. Jervis, who had begun his career as an "axeman," chopping trees to clear a path for construction on the Erie Canal, had quickly risen to supervisor before the canal's completion. Sharp-minded and practical, he had visited John Stevens's locomotive and had been impressed with what he saw. So in 1828 he sent his bright young assistant, Horatio B. Allen, off to England. There, under Jervis's orders—before the famous Rainhill trials of Stephenson's Rocket engine and before the Liverpool and Manchester line was completed—he bought four locomotives for experiment on the Delaware and Hudson. The locomotives, the America, the Stourbridge Lion, and the Delaware and the Hudson, began arriving in 1829.

On August 8, 1829, in a frightening test run across a rickety wooden bridge and around a sharp curve, the seven-ton Stourbridge Lion became the first English steam locomotive to travel on a track in America. Allen himself stood at the throttle, as he later told in this account, written in 1884:

> When the time came, and the steam was of the right pressure, and all was ready, I took my position on the platform of the locomotive alone, and with my hand on the throttle-valve handle said: "If there is any danger in this ride it is not necessary that the life and limb of more than one should be subjected to that danger."
>
> The locomotive, having no train behind it, answered at once to the movement of the hand; . . . soon the straight line was run over, the curve was reached and passed before there was time to think as to its not being passed safely, and soon I was out of sight in the three miles' ride alone in the woods of Pennsylvania. I had never run a locomotive nor any other engine before; I have never run one since.

Meanwhile, in 1827, the State of Maryland had chartered the first American railroad line, the Baltimore and Ohio Railroad Company, while South Carolina chartered the South Carolina Canal and Railroad Company. The B&O opened to much fanfare in 1830 with regularly scheduled trips between Baltimore and Ellicott's Mills, Maryland. Although that same year the B&O had also run the Tom Thumb, a tiny experimental locomotive built by American Peter Cooper, it relied in those early years on horse-drawn cars and experimental "sail-cars" to provide regular service on its tracks. One of its more curious experiments was a horse-treadmill arrangement. Literally "horse-powered," this train featured a large horse walking on a treadmill inside the lead car. The treadmill turned the wheels and powered the train. The 13-mile trip took an hour and a half with passengers seated on both sides of the car, facing, logically enough, away from the horse. The experiment came to an ignominious end after what may have been the first passenger-train accident: The horse/treadmill

car, filled with newspapermen, ran into a cow, tossing the passengers out of the train and down a steep hill.

A few years later a widely used history text of the time gave this account of those early days:

> But the most curious thing at Baltimore is the railroad. I must tell that there is a great trade between Baltimore and the States west of the Allegheny Mountains. The western people buy a great many goods at Baltimore, and send in return a great deal of western produce. There is, therefore, a vast deal of travelling back and forth, and hundreds of teams are constantly occupied in transporting goods and produce to and from market.
>
> Now, in order to carry on all this business more easily, the people are building what is called a railroad. This consists of iron bars laid along the ground, and made fast, so that carriages with small wheels may run along upon them with facility. In this way, one horse will be able to draw as much as 10 horses on a common road. A part of this railroad is already done, and if you choose to take a ride upon it you can do so. You will mount a car something like a stage, and then you will be drawn along by two horses, at the rate of 12 miles an hour.

Meanwhile, hoping to make Charleston, South Carolina a major seaport by bringing overland transportation to its docks, the South Carolina Canal and Railroad Company decided, after horse and sail-car experiments of its own, to run only steam locomotives on its line when completed. The decision was prompted by the advice of its new chief engineer, none other than Horatio Allen.

Not only had Allen fallen in love with the big, noisy steam locomotives he had brought from England, but he recognized their power. The short trip he had made on the Stourbridge Lion had convinced him of its might (although the Delaware and Hudson had retired the English locomotive almost immediately because it was too heavy for its tracks). Allen joined the SCC&RR in time to convince them that steam was the key to future transportation power.

On Christmas Day, December 25, 1830, after a series of trial runs, the Best Friend of Charleston, built for the SCC&RR by the West Point Foundry of New York City, became the first American-built steam locomotive in regular service in the United States. The small locomotive, weighing less than four tons, pulled two high-sided covered cars in which passengers sat on bare wooden bench-like seats. It puffed away at nearly 20 miles an hour.

The DeWitt Clinton, the first train operated in New York State, made its first trip August 9, 1831. Association of American Railroads

The Best Friend's glory days were short-lived, however. After only a half year of regular service it exploded when a fireman, bothered by the hissing of escaping steam from the engine, tied down its exhaust valve. The fireman was killed and the locomotive almost completely destroyed. Allen, however, had a second engine ready to go, and the West Point took to the tracks without any major interruption in service. In a smart public relations move, Allen put a protective barrier car, loaded down with heavy bales of cotton, between the engine and the four passenger cars the West Point pulled.

While it did offer some degree of safety and security, Allen's barrier car wasn't really needed. By now it seemed nothing could disenchant the public with steam locomotives. The Baltimore and Ohio gave up its experiments and converted to steam in 1831. That same year it introduced the first eight-wheel passenger car to the world (the first passenger cars had often looked more like four-wheeled stagecoaches than today's railroad cars) and began to cast about for the best way to give a little more comfort to the passengers by adding springs to the car. Other lines throughout the states were being planned or under construction.

Symbolic of this sudden about-face by the public and moneyed interests in favor of steam locomotives over canals, a group in upstate New York called the Mohawk and Hudson began building a railroad that would openly challenge the Erie Canal. The line, which later would become the first link in the New York Central System, inaugurated service in December 1831. Its chief engineer was ex-canal builder and railroad convert John B. Jervis, and its first steam locomotive was provocatively called the De Witt Clinton after the Erie Canal's prime supporter. Carrying traffic between Albany and Schenectady, the Mohawk and Hudson cut the distance from a long and winding 40-mile trip at four miles an hour by canal boat to a speedy and more or less direct 17-mile route by railroad track.

As later described by spectator William H. Brown in his book *The First Locomotives in America*, that first trip of the De Witt Clinton was an exciting, if uncomfortable, event:

How shall we describe that start, my readers? It was not that quiet, imperceptible motion . . . of the present day. Not so. There came a sudden jerk, that

12

bounded the sitters from their places, to the great detriment of their high-top fashionable beavers, from the close proximity to the roofs of the cars. This first jerk being over, the engine proceeded with considerable velocity for those times, when compared with stage coaches, until it arrived at a water station, when it suddenly brought up with jerk No. 2, to the further amusement of some of the excursionists. . . .

In a short time the engine (after frightening the horses attached to all sorts of vehicles filled with the people from the surrounding country, congregated all along at every available position near the road . . . [and] after causing innumerable capsizes and smash-ups of the vehicles and the tumbling of the spectators in every direction) arrived at the head of the inclined plane at Schenectady, amid the cheers and welcomes of thousands.

By this time the Stevens name once again had appeared in the forefront of American railroad building. The Camden and Amboy Railroad, which John

Stevens's sons Robert and Edwin had fought to build, was completed in 1832. The first 26 miles, between Bordentown and Amboy, New Jersey were completed in 1832. Its final link, between Bordentown and Camden, was opened the following year. The C&A, linked up with a system of ferry boats and steamboats, joined the bustling cities of New York and Philadelphia by rail and water. The president of the line and its chief engineer was young Robert Stevens. Robert, it turned out, was just as industrious and inventive as his father. Robert Stevens not only brought the English-built locomotive the John Bull to the United States but also invented the modern T-shaped American rail design, replaced the wooden track with iron and added wooden cross-ties instead of stone slabs to keep them in place. He is also credited with creating the "hook-headed railroad spike" now used throughout the world.

The "cowcatcher" was also developed during the early days of the Camden and Amboy to ward off accidents like the one suffered during the B&O's ill-fated horse-treadmill experiment. A mechanic

The John Bull locomotive. Association of American Railroads

named Isaac Dripps, who had to reassemble the John Bull without any instructions from its English makers, added the device to the front of the engine. Unfortunately for the cows Dripps's first design was a simple arrangement of two sharp iron spears that impaled any stubborn beasts that failed to move out of the way. Eventually, however, he evolved a more humane approach, finally designing the familiar V-shape cowcatcher seen on most early steam engines.

Railroads had unquestionably arrived in America. And while canals continued to boom in upstate New York, Pennsylvania and elsewhere, travelers and shippers had begun to recognize their relative limitations. Canals froze over and became useless during the cold north Atlantic winters; railroads could continue to run through snow, sleet and ice. Canals were more expensive and slower to build, and rugged terrain made for nearly insurmountable construction problems. And transportation by canal was agonizingly slow. Railroads, both travelers and merchants began to think, could go anywhere, both economically and rapidly.

3

TRAVEL TRANSFORMED:
RAILROAD NETWORKS REPLACE CANALS
1833–1860

PIONEER LINES

The railroad boom had begun.

In 1830 there were only 23 miles of operating railroad track. By the mid-1830s more than 1,000 miles had been laid and put to use. Driven by their intense competition for the business of increasingly prosperous communities just inland, the cities along the Atlantic coast rushed to charter railroads to connect them. The state of Massachusetts alone chartered three in 1830—the Boston and Lowell, the Boston and Providence, and the Boston and Worcester—to extend like spokes of a wheel from the Boston hub. In 1833 it began another, the Western Railroad, to connect Worcester with Albany. Along these routes valuable western produce could be brought to New England far more quickly than competing canal operators could move it. And by return trip New England manufacturers could send their products to inlanders. Just about everywhere a state, city, promoter or engineer thought new lines were needed they began to ribbon out across the land.

The southern states had also joined the boom. In 1831 the South Carolina Canal and Railroad became the first railway line to carry the U.S. mail. By 1833 the SCC&RR had laid over 136 miles of track into the rich southern cotton belt to become the longest railroad in the world. And when upstate Georgia towns chartered a line to connect with the railroad at Charleston, in 1833 the city of Savannah, fearing loss of trade, began building the Central of Georgia. Both railroad companies then talked the state into chartering an extension line to the west called the Western and Atlantic.

In 1834 the Utica and Schenectady started to lay track running parallel to the Erie Canal for 78 miles—in direct competition with the nine-year-old waterway. Like the Mohawk and Hudson before it, the Utica and Schenectady line formed the beginnings of the mighty New York railroad network that would later become the New York Central System.

On August 25, 1835 the B&O formally opened its branch connecting Baltimore with Washington, D.C., the first to run to the nation's capital. Although it had been slow to convert to steam, in the colorful citywide celebration the B&O presented a proud procession of four spanking-new steam engines, the George Washington, John Adams, Thomas Jefferson and James Madison. The B&O's service into Washington also offered the first railroad car fitted out with a special

The Thomas Viaduct, built by the B&O Railroad in 1835, still serves railroad traffic in the 1990s. B&O Railroad Museum

compartment for carrying mail. By 1838 Congress had designated all parts of the rapidly expanding railroad systems as postal routes.

Railroad construction slowed for a couple of years during the Panic of 1837, when Americans suddenly lost confidence in the economy and economic depression resulted, but the pace soon picked up again. By 1840 the railroads had laid track across as many miles as the canalers had dug canals.

Following the success of the Mohawk and Hudson, nine different lines run by nine separate companies had sprung into operation in New York State by 1842. Together they created a railroad link between the Great Lakes and Boston.

Every Middle Atlantic and New England state, with the sole exception of Vermont, had some form of railway, either steam- or horse-powered, in operation. The western states of Kentucky, Ohio and Indiana had plans on the drawing board. Rail, it was said now, was the cheapest and fastest way to go.

Over half of the "going" was done by passengers in the first few years. Not only was rail travel at least five times faster than travel by canal, but it was new and it

drew crowds of adventurous travelers. In its first year of operation alone, the little B&O carried 80,000 passengers along its 13-mile track. The SCC&RR made its 136-mile run in about 12 hours, for which passengers paid 5 cents a mile. Prior to its completion, a single two-seated stage had handled all the passenger traffic between Charleston and Hamburg in three trips a week. But in the first six months of 1835, the SCC&RR carried 15,959 passengers, who paid a total of more than $53,000 for tickets—a phenomenal increase in traffic and a tidy profit for the railroad.

All this enthusiasm survived despite the very real deterrents of discomfort, inconvenience and disorganization. Most of the passenger cars were still shaped like the traditional stagecoach, equipped with wheels and simply joined together. The engines bellowed and belched and smoke and sparks flew. The seats were hard and uncomfortable and timetables nonexistent.

Charles Dickens, who toured the United States in 1842, described the railroad cars he rode on as "like shabby omnibuses, but larger: holding 30, 40, 50 people. The seats," he continued,

Connecting Places

CHICAGO, HEART OF THE HEARTLAND

Located on Lake Michigan at the mouth of the Chicago River, in 1673 the site that would later become Chicago was visited by two French-Canadian explorers. At that time Louis Joliet and Father Jacques Marquette already foresaw the possibilities of the area as a great transportation center. But the first permanent settlement didn't spring up until about 1790, more than 100 years later, and when Chicago became incorporated as a city in 1837 the population stood at only a little over 4,000.

Chicago's location, however, promised rapid and dramatic growth from then on. Sometimes called "the city that had to be," its unique location is a natural point of convergence for the great midwestern prairie, the Great Lakes and the Chicago River. Even before the first railroad tracks ever reached it, Chicago had already become a major American port. Joliet and Marquette's vision began to become a reality on completion of a canal in 1848 linking the headwaters of the Chicago River, a part of the Great Lakes system, with the Des Plaines River, a part of the Mississippi River system. Once in operation, the Michigan and Chicago Canal opened up a direct link between the North Atlantic and the Gulf of Mexico, immediately making Chicago a major shipping gateway. In a few short years the port's docks were handling more ships each day than the combined traffic of its half-dozen closest competitors, including New York City.

When the railroads arrived, the addition of connections by land transformed the city into the nation's greatest transportation hub. The first train from the East entered Chicago over the Northern Indiana Railroad in 1852. By 1860 Chicago boasted 11 different railroad lines and had become the country's main freight transfer point. The construction of the nation's first transcontinental railroad, opening up the West in 1869, brought yet more traffic into the city. Wheat, cattle, people and hogs flowed to and through Chicago from all directions, filling its terminals, stockyards, slaughterhouses and ports. Factories, blast furnaces and packing plants sprang up, and even the disastrous Chicago Fire of 1871 couldn't deter the great city's growth.

Chicago, where lakes, rivers and railroads met in prosperous harmony, had truly become the heartbeat of America's heartland. Today more than 3 million people call Chicago home, and the "Windy City" on the lake remains unchallenged as the cultural and economic center of the Midwest.

instead of stretching end to end, are placed crosswise. Each seat holds two persons. There is a long row of them on each side of the caravan, a narrow passage up the middle, and a door at both ends. In the centre of the carriage, there is usually a stove, fed with charcoal or anthracite coal; which is for the most part red-hot. It is insufferably close; and you see the hot air fluttering between yourself and any other object you may happen to look at, like the ghost of smoke.

The ride itself he describes as wild and pell-mell,

. . . on, on, on—tears the mad dragon of an engine with its train of cars; scattering in all directions a shower of burning sparks from its wood fire; screeching, hissing, yelling, panting; until at last the thirsty monster stops beneath a covered way to

drink, the people cluster round, and you have time to breathe again. . . .

The system wasn't very well organized either. No one was quite sure who was in charge of the train. Was it the conuctor taking tickets or the locomotive engineer sitting in his cab? Many a passenger was stranded because an engineer decided that he might be late for supper and so it was time to go—a little ahead of schedule. To complicate matters even further, some people felt that a railway track should be like any other road. If you could build your own locomotive, they reasoned, you should just be able to pop it on or off and ride wherever you wanted.

Yet railroad fever was striking the nation.

And the railroad was changing from a useful novelty to big business.

Focus on Economics

HOW TO FINANCE A RAILROAD IN THE 1850S

Building a railroad, even in the 19th century, was a costly operation, and figuring out how to finance the undertaking proved highly complex.

Before 1860 about three-fourths of all money used for railroad construction came from private investors—some $800,000 in the 1850s alone. Local merchants, businessmen and farmers in areas where a railroad planned to build its tracks put up the money, hoping to profit when the iron horse finally began puffing across their lands and through their towns. Usually subscribers could put up their money in installments—known as calls—as the funds were needed for the various phases of construction. And a railroad could begin actually to pay for itself, once early sections were complete.

In sparsely populated or poorer districts, though—especially in the West—stocks were harder to sell. There, railroad builders often used bonds, backed by the railroad line's property, to raise the money they needed. Investors from New England and even Europe put up the funds, often using stock to maintain control.

But eventually nearly all the railroads running from the East Coast to the Midwest had to turn to state and local governments for financial help. Most of these railroads were financed partly by private funds and partly through government aid—amounting to as much as 25 to 30% of the total cost (still considerably less than government involvement with canals, however). Towns, counties and states made loans and invested in railroad stock. They afforded the railroads special privileges, such as tax-exempt status or the right to condemn property. And in some cases the railroads became public corporations.

For years, though, the federal government—waylaid by canal interests and southern and eastern votes—kept out of the railroad business. Finally in 1850 Congress passed the Illinois Central Land Grant Bill, which granted land to the Illinois Central Railroad in a complex checkerboard pattern along its right-of-way. The ICRR mortgaged the land to raise money or sold parts of it as farmland, yielding up $23.4 million for construction. The grant was such a success all around—stimulating settlement and farming in the area as well as railroading—that further land grants were made—20 million additional acres in the 1850s and many more after the Civil War. In return the federal government received free mail rates and government traffic on the railroads up to 1946, saving the U.S. government a total of $1 billion over the next 96 years.

MAKING THE CONNECTIONS

By the 1840s literally hundreds of little railroad lines, called "short lines," were in the planning stages or already running from city to city, city to town, town to mill, mill to port, just about wherever a needed connection could be made. The names told the story—the New York and Harlem, the Utica and Schenectady, the Saratoga and Schenectady, the Portsmouth and Roanoke. North and south, east and heading west, there was always a call for a railroad. And there was always someone, it seemed, to answer that call. In 1840 the nation had close to 3,000 miles of laid track. By 1848, 6,000 miles of track had been laid—though nearly all of it east of the Appalachians.

Not all of the lines prospered, though. Some early enterprises bloomed and withered within a few years. Others were stillborn, promoted by fast talkers who collected startup money from groups of hopeful citizens and then disappeared mysteriously to parts unknown.

All, though, were created out of dreams and promises—the dreams and promises of making connections, of tying separate communities together by track, of moving people and goods cheaply and efficiently along that track.

By the middle of the 1840s, freight traffic had surpassed passenger traffic as the railroad's main business. And although passenger traffic would continue to be important to the railroads for many years, freight would quickly make the railroad the economic backbone of America.

HEADING TOWARD THE MIDWEST

The early 1850s saw the railroads continuing to stretch toward the profitable markets of the Midwest. By the beginning of that decade, 9,000 miles of railroad track stretched across the land. By 1860 laboring work teams would have laid 30,636 miles of track.

The NY and Erie (later known as the Erie) opened the first direct-through line from the East in 1851, running from Piermont on the Hudson River to Dunkirk on Lake Erie. Farther west, the first train from the East entered Chicago over the Northern Indiana Railroad in 1852, completing the connection from Detroit. The Ohio River was reached from the east at Pittsburgh by the Pennsylvania Railroad, and the pioneer Baltimore and Ohio stretched out to Wheeling (in what is now West Virginia) on the Ohio River that same year.

In 1853 the Chicago, Rock Island and Pacific reached Rock Island, Illinois—the first rail route between the eastern seaboard and the Mississippi River. And in 1857 the Memphis and Charleston opened the first southern route from the eastern seaboard to the Mississippi when it reached Memphis, Tennessee. A "middle route" was also established in the same year when the Cincinnati and Baltimore Railroad connected East St. Louis with Cincinnati and Baltimore.

Most of the major railroad lines east of the Mississippi had been laid by the late 1850s, with practically no railroad construction yet west of the great river. One of the longest railroads in the world, the Illinois Central System, completed in 1856, stretched over 700 miles in the shape of a giant Y from Dubuque, Iowa in the northwest and Chicago in the northeast, joining in Centralia and continuing on to Cairo in the south. A precursor of the great boom to come, the Illinois Central—aided by the federal Illinois Land Grant Act of 1850 (see box)—helped open up the vast and fertile farmland of central Illinois.

By 1855, for a $20 to $30 ticket, you could travel from the midwestern cities of St. Louis or Chicago to the Atlantic seaboard in 48 hours. At the time of the B&O's historic first run 25 years earlier, the same trip would have taken two to three weeks.

BUILDING "THE WORK OF THE AGE"

In retrospect, the great speed with which railroaders covered the land with tracks belies the effort it actually took. The great New York and Erie Railroad, for example, took more than 18 years—filled with sweat, toil, strife and financial crisis—to complete. Little was known about railroad building when the New York and Erie was begun in 1833, and many decisions made in its early construction turned out to be costly mistakes. The gauge (or width between the rails), for example, was set at 6 feet—although most American railroads were using a 4-foot-8-inch gauge. In this way, New Yorkers reasoned, other railroads would be prevented from tying on to the Erie and draining traffic away from the state. Hundreds of miles of track had to be relaid in 1878 to correct the mistake.

Original plans also called for building the entire

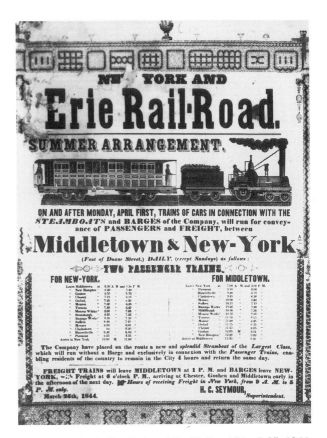

Poster issued by the New York and Erie Railroad March 25, 1844, shortly after the Erie began service to Middletown, New York. Association of American Railroads

railroad from the Hudson to Lake Erie on piers. The company president, Eleazar Lord, believed that an elevated railroad would be impervious to snowdrifts, washouts and grading problems. Surrounding farmers sold the railroad thousands of feet of oak piling, and crews of 13 men manned each of eight "Crane's Patent Pile Driving Machines." At a cost of $750,000, they drove 100 miles of piling at the western end of the line, but the idea was finally abandoned as impractical and the track was never laid on the piles.

From the start, the New York and Erie was undercapitalized—only 5% of the original subscriptions were paid—leaving the railroad short of cash at the outset. A disastrous fire in New York City ruined many NY & Erie subscribers, and the Panic of 1837 bankrupted many more. Work interruptions for shortage of funds were more the rule than the exception over the coming years. When the company ran out of money again in 1842, the town of Middletown, which had counted on becoming a railroad town, actually paid for construction of the remaining nine miles into town.

After a three-year hiatus, the State of New York came to the rescue, forgiving the NY & Erie's $3 million debt to the state. With the additional help of a new issue of $3 million in stock, the New York and Erie was ready to build in earnest at exactly the time when thousands of Irish immigrants were fleeing the potato famine of '45 and looking for work in the United States. The great 450-mile line, soon to be known as "The Work of the Age," would owe its existence to these hard-working, sinewy and daring (if sometimes boisterous) track crews. Driven hard by the Erie contractors, they hauled rails and ties, pounded spikes and blasted away mountainsides. Along the Delaware, they descended in baskets down the perpendicular cliffs to chip holes in the rock, tamp in the blasting powder, light the fuse and signal to be hauled back up. The dangerous job claimed many lives. The Work of the Age was finally finished in 1851, and the first through train ran on May 14, 1851.

Both before and after its completion, the line saw many firsts. The question of who was in charge of a train on the NY and Erie came to a head in 1842 when Ebenezer Ayres, the conductor, rigged a signal for stopping the train so nonpaying passengers could be put off. (It was the conductor's job to collect fares once the train was on its way, and some roustabouts were quick to see that they could get at least as far as the next station whether they had paid or not.) When engineer Abe Hammil, with a who's-running-this-train? attitude, refused to observe Ayres's signal, the feisty conductor decked Hammil and settled the ques-

tion, at least for the NY & Erie. Other lines soon followed suit, assigning authority to the conductor over the engineer.

The Erie also led the early railroads in another practical step toward establishing order. While Samuel B. Morse (1791–1872) sent his first long-distance telegraphic message over a line strung along the B&O right-of-way in May 1844, it was Charles Minot, newly appointed general superintendent of the Erie, who first put Morse's invention to work controlling trains in 1851. While riding a westbound train, Minot became impatient waiting for a tardy eastbound train to arrive. Having already recognized the potential of the telegraph for operating trains, he had convinced young Ezra Cornell (whose resulting enterprise became the New York & Western Union Telegraph) to string lines along the Erie tracks. Telegraph terminals were stationed at train depots along the way. So, on this day at Turner's Station (now Harriman, New York), Minot strode into the telegraph office, wired ahead to the next depot, at Goshen, to establish that the eastbound had not yet arrived, and then sent this order:

> To Agent and Operator at Goshen:
> HOLD EASTBOUND TRAIN UNTIL FURTHER ORDERS
>
> Charles Minot, Supt Erie

When the engineer of Minot's westbound train refused categorically to "run by that thing," Minot took over the train and proceeded safely to Goshen and then on to two more stations up the road—having wired ahead at each depot—before finally meeting the tardy eastbound a full hour later. According to railroad historian Stewart H. Holbrook, this concept of dispatching trains by telegraph would be "unquestionably the greatest single step taken by railroads in their formative era."

TYING THE SHORT LINES TOGETHER

A quick glance at a map showing the railroad lines east of the Mississippi in the early and mid-1850s would show a giant spiderweb of railroad tracks touching just about all major cities, towns and ports. A closer look, though, would reveal that the spiderweb was not smooth and continuous but was broken in many parts.

Typical were the 10 lines in New York State that served to link Boston with the Great Lakes. For the casual or commercial traveler, the journey was fraught with frustration and anxiety. Each of the short lines maintained its own often erratic schedule, issued its own "tickets" and made little or no effort to coordinate with each other. Passengers themselves had to carry their personal luggage from one line to the other. And passengers would often make a tiring trek from one station to another only to find no train waiting, or even expected, on the "connecting" line. Any long trip became a long, torturous nightmare for weary passengers.

For upstate New York the problem was solved in 1853 when New York short lines connected end to end, merging into one, long, major line, the New York Central. The move was a historic event in railroad history, a decision that would change the complexion of railroads forever. The NYC would go on expanding and merging in the next few years to become one of the nation's greatest and most powerful railroad lines.

In the few years before the Civil War, such mergers and consolidations of short lines into longer ones made the railroad the dominant form of transportation in the United States. These mergers and consolidations made for much more efficient service for the railroad's customers. They also consolidated the railroad's power. Now definitely "Big Business," railroads had begun to attract the enthusiasm not just of pioneers and dreamers but "money men" as well, investors and speculators who saw immense profits to be made in the big new systems.

The great profits to be made, in fact, along with public enthusiasm and lack of effective controls led to many unfortunate abuses. The force behind the great New York Central merger was a banker and iron manufacturer named Erastus Corning. Basically an honest railroad man, as president of the Utica and Schenectady he had refused any salary in exchange for exclusive rights to supply iron to the railroad. His practices came under scrutiny by an investigating committee, which exonerated him, but commented all too clairvoyantly, "the practice of buying articles for the use of the Railroad Company from its own officers might in time come to lead to abuses of great magnitude." By 1860 financial crookedness had already begun to infect the railroad industry, with inside trading on Wall Street, officers of companies issuing themselves phony stock, officer-owned construction companies bleeding assets and other blatant abuses. By 1860 men

such as Daniel Drew, Jim Fisk and Jay Gould had already taken over the great Erie Railroad and started the greedy manipulations that would ultimately lead to its financial destruction after the Civil War.

Competing with the New York Central for the title of the nation's greatest early railroad, the Pennsylvania Railroad began in 1846. The Pennsylvania State Legislature, disenchanted with the state's disjointed transportation system, chartered the "Pennsy," as it would later be nicknamed. The Pennsy's first task was to connect Harrisburg, the capital of Pennsylvania, with Pittsburgh. The existing route was a disastrously roundabout conglomeration of canals and rail lines that "took the steam" out of both engines and passengers before the journey was finished.

Shortly after opening in 1850 the Pennsy expanded and began buying up other existing railroads in the state. There were a lot to be bought. The short-line railroad boom during the late 1830s had given Pennsylvania more miles of railroad track than any other state in the nation. The historic Camden and Amboy was one of the earliest to be swallowed by the Pennsy, and such other pioneer lines as the Philadelphia and Columbia and the Germantown and Norristown quickly followed, as did dozens of less well-known short lines extending almost haphazardly across the state. By 1852 the Pennsylvania Railroad had established a line from Philadelphia across the mountains to Pittsburgh. The Pennsy quickly became a gigantic transportation network, consolidated and organized by the line's chief engineer, John Edgar Thomson, who planned and laid new tracks while incorporating the new acquisitions. He executed his vision so well that the Pennsy also built a solid reputation as one of the smoothest operations in the country.

The creation of the New York Central and Pennsylvania railroads seemed to mark an end to the age of trial and error for American railroads. The pioneer days were over. These networks of steel with their hurtling locomotives and clanking passenger and freight cars were fast coming to play important roles in the nation's economy and history.

In fact, the enormous spurt of railway construction had already made a telling impact in the mid-1800s. In a serendipitous meshing of trends, the influx of immigrants (providing cheap labor and eager settlers) combined with land grant offerings (such as those to the Illinois Central) to spur settle-

Trains and Dates

RAILROAD FEVER FACTS
1833–1860

1833   June 6. Andrew Jackson becomes the first U.S. President to travel by rail, on the B&O line between Ellicott's Mills, Maryland and Baltimore.

October 1. South Carolina Canal and Railroad Company completes its 136-mile line from Charleston to Hamburg on the Savannah River just across from Augusta, Georgia.

1835   August 25. The B&O opens its branch to Washington, D.C.

1836   Louis Wernwag builds a bridge across the Potomac for the B&O at Harper's Ferry (now in W. Virginia).

1837   Panic of 1837 slows railway construction; Illinois authorizes 1,300 miles of railroad construction.

1838   Congress designates all railroad systems as postal routes.

1840   3,000 miles of railroad track already have begun to connect parts of the nation.

A wooden railroad bridge over Catskill Creek in New York collapses, causing the first American fatality in a railroad bridge accident.

1844   Samuel B. Morse sends world's first telegram over a telegraph line strung along the B&O right-of-way.

1845   First iron-truss bridge in the United States is built by the Philadelphia and Reading Railroad near Philadelphia.

1848   Now a national landmark, the Starrucca Viaduct is built for the NY and Erie Railroad by a crew of 800 men at a cost of $320,000. It is the first American bridge with concrete piers.

1849   The Pacific Railroad Company, the first railroad west of the Mississippi, is chartered.

1850   The Pennsylvania Railroad opens.

May 14. Federal land grants to states are authorized to aid development of a railroad line from Lake Michigan extending 450 miles across New York State after 18 years of stop-start construction.

1851   July 1. The first known refrigerated car in the United States carries eight tons of butter from Ogdensburg, New York to Boston.

September 22. At Turner's Station (now Harriman), New York: First recorded use of telegraph for dispatching trains.

1852   May 21. A Northern Indiana Railroad train is the first to enter Chicago from the East (Detroit).

The Pennsylvania Railroad reaches the Ohio River at Pittsburgh.

The B&O reaches the Ohio at Wheeling.

December 9. First run west of the Mississippi, a five-mile trip made by the locomotive The Pacific from St. Louis to Cheltenham.

1853   Erastus Corning consolidates eight short lines between Albany and Buffalo, creating the New York Central system.

The Chicago, Rock Island and Pacific Railroad is the first to establish a rail route from the eastern seaboard to the Mississippi River.

As the trend toward westward movement continues, Congress authorizes a survey for the transcontinental railroad.

1855   John Roebling completes a railroad suspension bridge at Niagara Falls.

1856   The Illinois Central system completes 700 miles of track.

First sleeping car patents issued, to T. T. Woodruff.

1857   The Memphis and Charleston Railroad opens the first southern rail route from the East Coast to the Mississippi.

The Cincinnati and Baltimore establishes a "middle" route from St. Louis to Cincinnati and Baltimore.

1859   The first Pullman sleeping car makes an overnight run from Bloomington, Illinois to Chicago.

---

ment and cultivation of the vast prairie resources. The railroads provided jobs for immigrants, fostered farming and brought unprecedented revenues to the seaports along the Atlantic. Meanwhile, intermediate centers such as Buffalo and Chicago developed along the ribbons of rail. The changes were dramatic and sudden.

The years from 1830 to 1860 had seen a tremendous shift in the direction and volume of American commerce. Once the Erie Canal was completed in 1825, farm produce that had once flowed down the Mississippi River to New Orleans moved westward instead, through the Great Lakes and the canal to New York. By 1851, western commerce on the Erie Canal was 20 times its 1836 volume. Like Philadelphia, other competing Atlantic seaports had seen the canal's advantage well ahead of its arrival and had tried to copy its success. The resulting canal boom saw a period of feverish canal building—but few brought much success to their hopeful builders. As a result, once railroads began to look viable, nothing could stop the ribbons of steel from stretching out across the land.

Within the five years between 1850 and 1855, the great prairies of the Midwest were transformed. In 1850 no railroad stretched as far as Chicago. Five years later Chicago was the terminus for 2,200 miles of track, with some six lines connecting to the Mississippi. Like a great magnet, the new giant of the Mid-

west pulled in nearly all trade in the valley north of St. Louis. Almost all the output from the surrounding prairie sped into Chicago aboard the Illinois Central and its feeder lines. From there many carloads continued east via railroad or across the Great Lakes and down the Erie Canal to the coast. Once the prairies, far from water transportation and empty of timber for building, had stood empty and unsettled. Now farmers and settlers poured in. In 1840 some 8,500 people lived in the three-county area northeast of Springfield, Illinois. Just 20 years later nearly four times as many people lived in the area, and they were producing more than nine times as much wheat as in 1840 and eight times as much corn.

Wherever it extended its tracks, the railroad stimulated real estate and investment banking. Its voracious need for iron encouraged mining, smelting and engine foundries.

And the cheap transportation introduced by railroads transformed the American economy. In the stiff competition for traffic, canal operators engaged in heavy price wars with the railroads, forcing fares down. The beneficiaries were American consumers. Hoping to draw off those cargoes that didn't have to be transported quickly, the Erie Canal dropped its rates by as much as two-thirds. The railroad retaliated, dropping the rate for shipping a bushel of wheat from Chicago to New York via railroad as low as 35 cents just

The decade 1850–1860 was a period of rapid railway expansion, characterized by the extension of many short lines. By 1860 the nation's railway network increased to a total of 30,626 miles. Association of American Railroads

before the Civil War. As a result, the center of American wheat production shifted to Illinois, Wisconsin and Indiana. Factory workers in New England could spread their tables with produce raised by farmers in Illinois. From west of the Appalachian "barrier," virtually impenetrable a few years before, came two-thirds of all the meat eaten in New York City.

The Panic of 1857 brought a brief collapse—Russian wheat, kept off the market during the Crimean War, came back and American wheat prices plummeted. As a result, agricultural expansion dropped off and the railroads suffered. But most areas recovered quickly. The economy, with railroads at its heart, seemed on the upswing again when a dark cloud forming on the horizon began to become more threatening. The Civil War—that strife-filled period when North fought bitterly against South—brought with it a new era for the nation's railroads, a period of loss and turmoil, with both sides using and destroying railroads to cripple the enemy.

4

RAILROADING FIGHTS A WAR
1859–1865

In 1859 and 1860 the strained relations between the agrarian South's policy of slavery and the industrial North's opposition to slavery culminated in the bloody War Between the States. And the nation's railroads found themselves caught up as key players in one of America's most tragic conflicts.

The southern lines would suffer the most.

By 1860 the southern states had completed an intricate network of railroads that tied together its major cities and agricultural centers. Three major connections carried east-west traffic. The first connection ran from the coast to Mississippi by way of a series of short lines or independents stretching from Charleston, South Carolina 755 miles to Memphis, Tennessee. The second stretched from the east to the southwest over 1,215 miles of rail from Alexandria, Virginia to Mobile, Alabama also by way of independents, and a third set of links tied Norfolk, Virginia on the coast to Memphis, Tennessee and the Mississippi River.

Three other major connections ran along the north-south route. A series of independents linked Richmond, Virginia by way of Wilmington, North Carolina to Sumter, South Carolina. The Mobile and Ohio Railroad ran from Meridian, Mississippi north as far as Columbia, Kentucky. And from the Gulf of Mexico, the New Orleans, Jackson and Great Northern Railway ran through Memphis and Jackson, Tennessee, north to Paducah, Kentucky on the Ohio River and then on to Cairo, Illinois, where it connected with the Illinois Central to carry passengers and freight on up to Chicago.

By the end of the war many of these lines would be severely damaged, some beyond repair. The South Carolina Railroad would be almost completely destroyed, the Mississippi Central left with only one depot intact and only three of its 30 locomotives in running order. The New Orleans, Jackson and Great Northern, once one of the South's best-equipped railroads, would lose over 500 freight cars, 33 passenger cars, and 47 locomotives, leaving only 36 freight cars, four passenger cars, and two locomotives in operation. Many of the short lines and independents would vanish completely.

For the railroads—especially the Baltimore and Ohio—the war began even before its official beginning on April 12, 1861, when Confederate troops fired upon Fort Sumter. Ironically, the B&O, a major target of southern aggression, became an early victim of northern passions during a famous "prewar" attack at Harper's Ferry, Virginia (now West Virginia). On October 16, 1859 the fiery abolitionist John Brown began a personal crusade against slavery by attacking the federal arsenal at Harper's Ferry. During the raid Brown also stopped the B&O's Wheeling-to-Baltimore Express, killing the station master and a train

Destruction of this Richmond, Virginia railroad station, pictured here in April 1865, was typical of the devastation suffered by southern railroads during four years of war. Association of American Railroads

porter. Brown was routed from Harper's Ferry, captured and executed, but his attack on the B&O demonstrated the deep involvement and crucial importance railroads would have for both sides during the war.

The B&O, a critical but vulnerable east-west link for the federal government, was in constant turmoil due to its location in the contested Potomac Valley. On May 25, 1861 Confederate troops set a blast under overhanging rocks to send them crashing down on the tracks near Point of Rocks, Maryland. Within a week two bridges at Buffalo Point, West Virginia were destroyed, and Confederate troops captured the trunk line from Point of Rocks to Cumberland. In June and July of that same year, Confederate troops raided the B&O yards at Martinsburg, West Virginia and confiscated 14 locomotives for use in the South. They destroyed and burned 42 others as well as 386 passenger and freight cars. Twenty-three bridges were also wrecked and many other locomotives derailed.

Martinsburg would become a target again in October 1862, when the recently repaired buildings, rolling stock, engine houses and machine stops would once again be attacked and destroyed. During this

raid the Confederate troops built gigantic bonfires with the B&O's railroad ties and used them to heat the rails, softening them enough to allow them to be literally wrapped and tied around trees so they couldn't be reused.

During the next few years the B&O would suffer continual attacks, including the destruction of 41 miles of track by Confederate troops led by General Stonewall Jackson. Under the changing tides of war, major sections of the line would be damaged by one side and then captured and repaired by the other—back and forth, back and forth—as the Potomac Valley belonged first to one side and then to the other.

Although the southern railroads and the vulnerable B&O suffered the worst physical damage during the war, not a railroad in the nation was unaffected in some way. Forces on both sides seized commercial railroad property and materials for use in their own strategic military railways, and for the first time in history railroads became valuable tools in the movement of troops and supplies. At one point General Daniel C. McCallum of the Union Army was able to transport 22,000 men along with mules, artillery and supplies the 1,168 miles from Washington, D.C. to Bridgeport, Alabama in only seven days. General William T. Sherman once said that without the support McCallum provided through his use of railroads, the Atlanta Campaign of 1864 "would have been impossible." And in the South, the South Carolina Railroad was used almost solely for troop and military supply transport.

Farther north, away from the scenes of battle, the eastern railroads boomed during the war years. Already largely responsible for the steady stream of goods that moved profitably between the East Coast and the Northwest and assured northwestern support for the Union, the eastern lines now carried even higher traffic loads. Farmers and businessmen preferred to avoid the dangers of shipping near the southern battle lines. Major southern ports such as New Orleans, which had been receiving 10 million bushels of grain annually from the Northwest, were cut off when the war virtually closed down all trade on the Mississippi River. Grain, like many other agricultural and mining goods, flowed steadily eastward

through the port of Chicago, further boosting profits and cementing allegiances.

Although the federal government occasionally commandeered some locomotives for use by the U.S. military, most ran privately, and for a profit. By the war's end many eastern lines that had been struggling before the conflict began had paid off their indebtedness and were showing a healthy profit. Still, many eastern lines were quick to grumble about lost profits when *any* of their rolling stock was commandeered. When Cornelius Vanderbilt complained about the military seizure of some of the New York and Harlem's cars and locomotives, he received this gentle but pointed lecture in an 1863 telegraphed reply from Secretary of War Edwin M. Stanton:

> Your letter of the nineteenth has just been rec'd. The engines referred to were seized by order of this department from an absolute and paramount necessity for the supply of the armies on the Cumberland. They are absolutely essential for the safety of those armies and the order cannot be revoked. Whatever damages your company may sustain the government

Soldiers destroying track during the Civil War. Association of American Railroads is responsible for but the military operations and the supply of arms at Chattanooga in the judgement of this department and no doubt also in your judgement are superior to every other consideration. . . . I hope then that you will not only throw no obstacle in the way of a speedy forwarding of these engines to Louisville but that you will use your well known energy in aid of the Government to hurry them forward.

Edwin M. Stanton
Secretary of War

Meanwhile, while some, although not all, of the northern railroads were grumbling about their profit margins, the battle for possession of the railroad lines continued in the South.

In a daring move in December 1862, General John H. Morgan led 4,000 Confederate troops in an attack on the Louisville and Nashville Railroad, 60 miles south of Louisville, at Upton, Virginia, a town held at that time by the Union Army. Called "the gut of the South" by President Lincoln, this critical route connected Nashville with Louisville, Frankfort, Lexington and the North. Morgan's raid was aimed directly at destroying this strategic Union avenue to Georgia. Descending on the Union troops protecting the line, Morgan took over the telegraph station to wire Union General Jeremiah Boyle at Louisville. Using the name of a Union commander, Morgan managed to gather information about the Union troops and confuse Boyle about Morgan's own location and strength. He then proceeded to capture and stockade dozens of railroad bridges from Upton to Shepherdsville to the northeast, stationing 500 to 700 men to secure and protect each one.

The most famous railroad raid in the South, though, was conducted by James J. Andrews, a civilian volunteer for the Union. The April 25, 1862 issue of *The Atlanta Confederacy*, a Georgia newspaper, described the event as "the most thrilling railroad adventure that has ever occurred on the American Continent." According to railroad historian Freeman Hubbard, the plan was "brilliantly planned and boldly carried out."

The daring raid began on April 12, 1862, when Andrews and 19 Union soldiers disguised themselves as southerners and boarded a northbound train at Marietta, Georgia. The train, a mixed passenger and freight, was pulled by a locomotive named the General. Among Andrews's men were two experienced railroad engineers, one from the Pittsburgh and Fort Wayne Railroad and the other from the Mobile and Ohio. Andrews's objective was to destroy a key Confederate rail connection between Chattanooga and Atlanta by burning the bridges on the single-tracked Western and Atlanta Railroad and cutting the telegraph lines along the way. The plan was to take over the train at Big Shanty, Georgia and make a run for the Union lines, leaving a trail of burning bridges behind and effectively cutting off Confederate forces at Chattanooga from Atlanta, one of their chief supply bases.

Big Shanty was deep in Confederate territory. At nearby Camp McDonald, 3,000 Confederate troops were training and the entire area was awash in Confederate gray. When the train pulled in for a breakfast stop, Andrews—dressed like a southern gentleman in beard, high silk hat, frock coat, white shirt, small bow tie and gray striped pants—climbed off with his men and joined the rest of the passengers milling around. Later stories said that Andrews had whispered orders to his men, reminding them not to fire unless it was absolutely necessary. Whether true or not didn't matter. There was no need for gunfire at that point. As the other passengers seated themselves for breakfast, Andrews and one of his men sauntered casually over to the engine. Along the way they had deftly pulled the coupling pin that attached the passenger cars and the heavy mail car to the box cars immediately behind the engine. As Andrews's men jumped aboard the box cars, Andrews and William Knight, one of the two Union engineers with the group of raiders, quickly boarded the locomotive and released its brakes. Knight opened the throttle and in a moment the eight-wheeled wood-burning engine was moving down the tracks.

"It was a moment of triumphant joy that will never return," William Pittenger, one of Andrews's raiders, later wrote. "Not a dream of failure shadowed my rapture. All had told us that the greatest difficulty was to reach and take possession of the engine, and after that success was certain."

Captain W. A. Fuller assumed that Confederate deserters had taken off with his engine—certainly he didn't imagine that Union soldiers could be anywhere in the area. But nevertheless, he was the conductor and it was his train that suddenly chugged off without him. In seconds he was out the door, pursuing the train on foot. His guess was that if the train had been commandeered by deserters, they would probably abandon it a few miles away. With his long, black beard flowing in the wind, Fuller tried to keep the train in sight as he ran along the tracks. It was a valiant

Focus on People

LINCOLN'S LAST JOURNEY

Defeated, General Robert E. Lee, commander of the Confederate Army, surrendered for the South at Appomattox, Virginia on April 9, 1865. The bloody war that had torn the nation apart was over. Echoes of that tragedy would linger for years, however, as the war-weary nation tried to piece itself back together.

Five days later President Abraham Lincoln attended a play at Ford Theater in Washington, D.C. Before the play was over that night, the man who had labored so hard and eloquently to heal the nation's wounds was himself fatally wounded, assassinated by the actor and fanatic John Wilkes Booth.

Lincoln's death stunned the nation. As James Russell Lowell, an American essayist and poet, wrote: "Never before that startled April morning did such multitudes of men shed tears for the death of one they had never seen as if with him a friendly presence had been taken from their lives, leaving them colder and darker."

On Friday, April 21, 1865 a special train carrying the body of the nation's fallen President pulled out of Washington, D.C. and began its melancholy journey to return the remains of Abraham Lincoln to his home in Springfield, Illinois. Painted entirely in black on the outside and draped in black throughout, it carried not only Lincoln's body but the remains of his son Willy, who had died in 1862 and had been temporarily interred in a Washington cemetery vault. The Lincolns had always planned to take Willy's body home to Illinois with them when Lincoln finished his term as President. Now, though, the bodies of father and son, accompanied by Lincoln's widow, Mary Todd Lincoln, and their two sons, Robert and Ted, made the mournful journey together.

The route covered 1,700 miles over 13 railroad lines and lasted 13 days. Some 26 different engines were used, including a series of pilot engines that traveled ahead to assure a clear track. Along the way, in towns and villages, the train stopped to allow over 1,500,000 people to view Lincoln's body. Nearly 7 million more stood silently along the tracks in the countryside, their heads bowed, as the funeral train crawled slowly by.

After the train stopped in Philadelphia, Lincoln's casket was taken to Independence Hall and solemnly displayed next to the Liberty Bell as the mourners passed by. To add to the melancholy of the occasion, a heavy downpour began shortly after the casket was returned to the train. Most of the rest of the journey was completed in a steady rain.

For the last leg of the journey, beginning at Alton, Illinois, the Chicago and Alton Railroad connected the Pioneer for Mrs. Lincoln's use. It was the first "sleeping car," with seats that converted to beds, to be built entirely by George Pullman, whose name would become synonymous with railroad sleepers and luxury rail travel.

Finally, at 9:00 A.M. on May 3, the black train arrived at its destination. The depot was draped in black and church bells rang throughout the night as the President's body was displayed for one last time at the state capitol. The next morning, under the still rain-darkened skies, Abraham Lincoln's body was placed to rest in a cemetery vault.

effort, but he was soon left behind as the engine picked up speed. Undaunted, Fuller continued his pursuit. Reaching Moon Station, two miles away, he first began to suspect Union sabotage when he discovered that the men on the commandeered train had stopped to steal track tools and telegraph wire.

While Fuller was making his discovery, his engineer, Jeff Cain, and Tony Murphy, the foreman at the Western and Atlantic's railroad shops, caught up with him. Fuller, Cain and Murphy quickly set a small push car on the tracks—the route by this time was mostly downhill—and continued their pursuit.

Andrews and his raiders in the meantime had begun to tear up sections of the track. Fuller, Crane and Murphy picked up the push car and walked it around the bad sections, then set it back on the tracks and continued relentlessly after the General. Pushing on to Acworth, they picked up two more men and some guns, and continued their chase. At Etowa, a few more miles down the line, Fuller and his men discovered that the raiders had made their first mistake. They had not sabotaged the locomotive Yonah, which was usually kept at the station. It was steamed up and ready to go. Pittenger later explained that Andrews had not wanted to attract more attention or cause alarm by disabling the Yonah. Deep in enemy territory, the raiders had hoped to go on unsuspected until all the oncoming trains had passed by. They had cut telegraph lines and continued posing as Confederates, convincing station employees along the way to supply them with fuel and water. What they didn't know about, and hadn't counted on, was that the General's determined conductor and his cohorts were fast closing in on them.

By now Fuller, joined by six more men and running the Yonah in reverse with the tender leading, was back on the chase, speeding at 60 miles an hour and closing.

At Kingston, Andrews impersonated a Confederate officer and persuaded the railroad men to cooperate by telling them he was carrying ammunition to Confederate General Pierre Beauregard, who was waiting for the delivery at Corinth. The station crew gave him a switch key and moved aside some freight trains that had been blocking his way.

Valuable time was lost, however, as the trains were moved to the siding. And, still unknown to Andrews, Fuller was closing the gap on him. Pulling into Kingston just four minutes after Andrews's departure, Fuller and his men leaped onto a locomotive that was positioned at the head of the blockade and continued the chase. Once again, though, Andrews and his men had started to tear up track. Abandoning their locomotive and again running on foot, Fuller and his men, who now numbered about 12, lucked upon a freight train moving in the opposite direction. Stopping it with a few gunshots fired in the air, Fuller explained the situation to the engineer, who recognized him. The engineer quickly backed his train into a siding, uncoupled the cars and pulled the engine back on to the right of way, heading back toward Chattanooga with Fuller and his band aboard.

Meanwhile, Andrews, exasperated, asked one of the train conductors why there was so much unscheduled oncoming train traffic. Ironically, the Union Army, he was told, had captured Huntsville and was said to be moving toward Chattanooga. In response, the Confederates were moving everything they could away from the Union's expected attack.

As the frustrated Andrews was getting this information, Fuller had quite literally scooped up a 12-year-

This 13-inch mortar, used by the federal artillery near Petersburg during the closing months of the war, weighed 17,000 pounds and was so heavy that it had to be mounted on a railroad car for easier movement. Association of American Railroads

---

Trains and Dates

CIVIL WAR TRAIN FACTS
1859–1865

1859 October 16. John Brown raids the U.S. arsenal at Harper's Ferry and attacks the B&O's Wheeling-to-Baltimore Express.

1861 Confederate soldiers make the first strategic use of the railroad in the Civil War by using the Manassas Cap Railroad to cross the Blue Ridge Mountains to the battle of Bull Run.

1862 April 12. James J. Andrews leads a band of 21 men in a daring attempt to steal a locomotive deep inside southern territory and destroy the rail connection between Atlanta and Chattanooga.

April–May. Bridge engineer Herman Haupt is hired by the U.S. War Department to rebuild vital bridges burned by the Confederates outside Richmond. He and his untrained crew built the 150-foot Ackacreek Bridge in 15 hours and the 400-foot Potomac Creek Bridge in nine days.

Confederates move the entire Army of the Tennessee, commanded by General Braxton Bragg, from one theater of war to another, from Tupelo, Mississippi to Chattanooga, Tennessee.

December 25. Confederate General John H. Morgan leads "Morgan's Raid" on the Louisville and Nashville Railroad, at that time under control of Union troops.

1863 September. Confederate General James Longstreet's Corps travels 835 miles by rail from Virginia to join in the Battle of Chickamauga near Chattanooga.

Union Colonel D. C. McCallum moves 22,000 men, artillery and supplies by rail from the Potomac to Bridgeport, Alabama, a total of 1,168 miles, in seven days.

1865 April 21. Abraham Lincoln's funeral train pulls out of Washington, D.C. for the long trip home to Springfield, Illinois.

---

old telegraph operator at Calhoun and wrote a wire for the Confederate general at Chattanooga:

> My train captured this a.m. in Shanty. Evidently federal soldiers disguised. They are heading for Chattanooga, probably with the idea to burn railroad bridges in their rear. If I do not capture them in the meantime, see that they do not pass Chattanooga.

The chase was narrowing, however. And soon, for the first time since the start of his pursuit, Fuller could see the General ahead.

At last Andrews became aware that he was being chased. Hoping to slow the pursuers down, he ordered his men to start uncoupling freight cars and leaving them on the track. Determined not to lose sight of the

General again, Fuller barely slowed down as he picked the abandoned cars up one by one and pushed them along ahead of his engine, while directing his engineer from the front of the cars. When he dropped the cars off at a siding at Resca, Fuller also dropped off the 12-year-old telegraph operator with instructions to send his message. Then he continued his chase.

Ahead, running for his life now in the General, Andrews had to abandon his plan to burn bridges. The day was rainy and wet, and his pursuers were just too close behind to give the raiders enough time to get fires started.

Andrews didn't entirely give up the idea of fighting with fire, though. After lighting a fire on one of the few freight cars still attached to the General, he uncoupled it and left the blazing car in the path of his

31

pursuers. Again Fuller, with his men following him, abandoned their locomotive and continued on foot.

This time, though, Andrews and his men on the General couldn't use the advantage to put more distance between themselves and their pursuers. The General was rapidly running out of fuel. At the throttle Knight, as he later wrote, felt helpless:

> There is little more to tell. Wilson had thrown the last stick of wood into the fire, and water was not showing on the gauge. Soon we were running only 25 miles an hour, then 20, then 15; and then came Andrews's last command: "Stop her, Knight! Scatter boys! It's every man for himself now!"

With the General abandoned, the end was inevitable. Still deep in Confederate territory, Andrews and his men had little chance on foot and, although Fuller, the most determined pursuer, didn't capture anyone, Andrews and his raiders were soon rounded up and the long chase of the General was finished.

Because they had impersonated Confederate soldiers, Andrews and seven of his men were hanged as spies. Brave to the end, Andrews declared, "I have often thought I would like to see what lies on the other side of the river Jordan."

The remaining 14 of Andrews's men were imprisoned. Eight managed to escape from their confinement while the remaining 6 were eventually traded back to the North in exchange for Confederate prisoners.

Fuller was honored by the Georgia legislature, which voted to give him a gold medal. But gold was so scarce that the medal was never made. He was fired at the end of the war, but later went to work for the Georgia Pacific.

In 1891 a statue honoring Andrews was erected at the National Cemetery at Chattanooga.

The Civil War finally ended in 1865 with Confederate General Robert E. Lee's surrender at Appomattox. For the railroads, the war left behind a new place in military history, a wide path of destruction (especially in the South) and (for the North) a legacy of growth and profit.

For the first time railroads had been used as a military tool for strategic movement of troops and supplies over long distances. Soldiers had been moved by train in a matter of days from one theater to bolster campaigns in another. And construction methods were so improved that new military railroads sprang into service almost overnight, traveling over quickly laid track and bridges built with lightning speed.

Southerners had seen too many northern railroads, such as the B&O, extended into their territory, and civilian parties set out to tear up ties and rails, torch bridges and blow up locomotives. Both sides burned stations, destroyed cars and engines, and disabled water tanks in each other's territory. The South, however, which began the war with a weaker railroad system—only about 9,000 miles of track compared to about 27,000 miles in the North—suffered the most. Drained of all its resources during the war, the South would be slow to recover. It would take 15 years before cotton growers would see a year of profits equal to what they had enjoyed in 1860, at the start of the war. Tobacco growers would not equal that year's profits until 1900. The railroads' devastation in the South greatly contributed to the crippling of the economy, and they too were slow to recover. Only 7,000 miles of track were built in the South between 1865 and 1879, compared to 45,000 miles of new track laid in the rest of the country.

In the North, the war years proved to be a time of growth and profit for railroads, which in general were better run and stronger than their southern counterparts. New England railroads, far from troop movement and the booming grain transportation market, saw the least growth, carrying mostly manufactured goods. In Pennsylvania the growing iron, coal and petroleum industries gave railroad profits a strong boost. And while western railroads carried the crops of the Great Plains to market, the north-south lines, such as the Illinois Central and the Cleveland, Columbus and Cincinnati, thrived on Union Army business. During each of the five years of war, the northern lines showed record profits with both freight tonnage and passenger traffic increasing as much as 100% on the Erie, Illinois Central and Pennsylvania railroads.

Overall, railroads and the country as a whole would see, in the years that followed the war, some of the most exciting expansion and growth ever enjoyed—a time of western movement, pioneering and adventure, a time when ribbons of steel and the iron horse would finally connect America from shore to shore. The day of the transcontinental railroad was about to dawn.

5

BUILDING A RAILROAD ACROSS AMERICA: THE CENTRAL PACIFIC BUILDS EASTWARD 1853–1869

The transcontinental railroad wasn't at all a new idea—some visionaries had been proposing such a project for a long time. As early as 1832 (when probably not more than 200 miles of rail had been laid anywhere in the country), one writer already envisioned a railroad project connecting New York and Oregon. His article appeared in a weekly newspaper called *The Emigrant*, published in Ann Arbor, Michigan. By 1844 New York merchant Asa Whitney proposed to the government that he build a line from Lake Michigan to the Columbia River. Whitney had traveled on railroads in England and, in a visit to China, had recognized the foreign trade opportunities to the Orient. He brought vision, economic savvy and political expertise to his proposal, and, backed by his argument that a transcontinental line would establish a rich trade link between the West Coast of the United States and the Orient, he actually won the approval of 17 states before running headlong into Senator Thomas Hart Benton of Missouri. Benton blocked the proposal, arguing that if a transcontinental railroad was to be built it should be constructed by the United States government, and should probably start at St. Louis on the Mississippi (not coincidentally the leading port of Benton's home state). The Benton proposal and its influential supporters effectively scut-

tled Whitney's plan, which ended up being tabled by Congress.

So during the 1840s, even as the network of rails connected more and more points in its vast spiderweb east of the Mississippi, the great challenge of extending rails from coast to coast remained unmet. The brouhaha over Whitney's plan, though, had begun to spark some genuine interest in the whole idea of a railroad to cross the continent. With the 1848 discovery of gold at Sutter's Mill in California, rail transport to the far West had become an even more attractive possibility. By 1853 Congress had set aside $150,000 and authorized a survey for a transcontinental railroad to the Pacific. Five different surveying teams set out to find the perfect route.

One Connecticut-born engineer, meanwhile, had also begun to have serious thoughts on the subject. In fact, Theodore D. Judah's closest associates came to consider him a fanatic when it came to the transcontinental railroad. The son of a New England clergyman, Judah had graduated from Rensselaer Polytechnic Institute and had gone to work immediately building railroads in New England and along the East Coast. In 1854 he trekked west to build the first railroad line in California, a short line from Sacramento to Folsom, the gateway to gold country in the

---

Trains and Dates

PUTTING RAILS THROUGH THE SIERRAS
1853–1869

1853   Congress authorizes a survey for the transcontinental railroad route.

1861   The "Big Four"—Stanford, Crocker, Huntington and Hopkins—agree to finance Theodore Judah's proposed Central Pacific Railroad.

1862   The Pacific Railway Act gives authority to the Union Pacific Railroad to build westward from Nebraska to meet the Central Pacific, which will build eastward from California.

1863   January 8. Ground-breaking for the CP at Sacramento.

Judah is forced out of the CP.

1866   More than 6,000 Chinese have been hired to help build through the Sierras.

November. The CP runs as far as Cisco, a five-hour, 94-mile trip from Sacramento.

1867   By late this year the CP has completed 15 tunnels and is through the Sierras.

1869   April 28. The CP crews win a $10,000 bet against the UP track layers, completing 10 miles and 200 feet of track in one day.

Sierra foothills. His route had taken him first by sailing ship to Central America, by a succession of stagecoaches to the Pacific Coast and then by ship again to San Francisco, with more stagecoaches to Sacramento, a few miles inland. It was a long, arduous journey, but the options—sailing the long way around Cape Horn, or making the entire voyage by slow wagon trains across the dangerous American prairie—weren't much more attractive. The journey convinced Judah that there had to be a better way to reach the Pacific coast.

With the successful completion of his Sacramento-Folsom line, Judah became even more convinced that a transcontinental railroad was not only needed but possible as well. The problems inherent in building a railroad line across the rugged Sierra Nevada range between California and Nevada were substantial. But Judah managed to get enough Californians interested to organize the Pacific Railroad Convention in 1859. The convention quite naturally selected Judah to be its spokesman, and he headed East again to present his arguments to politicians and potential backers.

However, if Judah had been hopeful during his long journey back east, his spirits quickly sank as he tried to approach eastern backers. Preoccupied with the steadily growing tensions between the North and the South over the problems of slavery, most people of influence refused to see him at all. Those who did questioned any railroad's ability to cross the Sierra Nevadas.

Discouraged, with his pockets empty, Judah again made the long trek west, determined now to seek backing from the westerners themselves. This time, to shoot down worries about the Sierra crossing in advance, he decided first to survey possible routes himself through the steep, treacherous mountain range. Judah spent the summer of 1860 in the Sierras with his surveying instruments and mountain gear, scouting for the best route across the rugged mountains. With the results of his survey in hand, he returned to San Francisco and renewed the effort to find backers for his proposed "Central Pacific Railroad."

Again, however, he met resistance. Although plenty of people liked the idea of a railroad and the benefits of a direct line to the east, no one seemed ready to risk money on the venture. In addition, some San Franciscans worried that if the railroad did manage to go through, it might endanger the city's economic importance as an ocean port.

Finally, though, one night in June 1861, after returning to Sacramento, Judah found his backers.

In a small room over a Sacramento hardware store, four wealthy merchants—Leland Stanford, Charles Crocker, Collis P. Huntington and Mark Hopkins—agreed to finance Judah's railroad.

Judah's dream was about to come true. His four new backers immediately sent him east to lobby for government support, and this time it worked. By now, after years of festering tension, the Civil War had broken out between the northern and southern states. Recently elected President, Abraham Lincoln recognized the importance of keeping California and its wealth solidly in the Union and in 1862 signed the Pacific Railroad act into law. The act decreed that two lines, with considerable government assistance, would connect to build the nation's first transcontinental railroad.

Judah's Central Pacific would begin building eastward from Sacramento, while another, the newly formed Union Pacific, would start at the Mis-

souri River and begin building westward toward Utah. As part of the act, Congress would also agree to give the railroads free land and the proceeds of bond sales to help in the initial construction. Both the Central Pacific and the Union Pacific were also given a 400-foot right-of-way across government lands on which they could build switchyards, stations and shops, and an additional 10 square miles of land for each mile of track completed.

Elated, Judah again returned to Sacramento. His elation, though, was not to last for long. In his absence his partners had already begun organizing and building their railroad—and their new careers. Theodore Judah had seen a railroad. His partners saw an empire. Newly elected governor of California, Leland Stanford had promised the voters the railroad would bring great wealth and prosperity—and he, along with the other three partners of what would come to be called the "Big Four," intended

This cut, located between Auburn and Newcastle, was one of the most difficult jobs of the early years of Central Pacific construction. Blasted to a depth of 85 feet, it was 800 feet long. Association of American Railroads

to get a big share of that wealth and prosperity. Judah was welcome to come along for the ride, as long as he agreed to remain blind to the Big Four's financial and political maneuvering as well as a little bit of chicanery. Seeing that there was big money to be made in railroads, the four were ready to move mountains to get at it. In fact, they had already managed just such a trick, persuading a geologist to declare that the foothills of the Sierra Nevadas actually started just outside of Sacramento (when in fact they are at least 31 miles away). Since the U.S. government subsidized $12,000 a mile on level ground and $48,000 a mile for laying track over the more difficult mountain terrain, the Big Four were already collecting a tidy sum by the time that Judah learned about the scheme.

Disillusioned, Judah immediately began arguing with his partners over this and similar issues, until finally, as he wrote in May 13, 1863 in a letter to a friend:

I cannot tell you in the brief space of a letter all that is going on, or of all that has taken place; suffice to say that I have had a pretty hard row to hoe.

I had a blow-out about two weeks ago and freed my mind, so much so I looked for instant decapitation. I called things by their right name and invited war; but councils of peace prevailed and my head is still on; but my hands are tied, however.

By summer the Big Four had forced Judah out, purchasing his interest for the sum of $100,000. It was the end of a dream for the visionary engineer. The railroad would be built, but it would not be his. Beaten, but determined to fight, he started east one more time. His last hope was that he could find enough new financial assistance to wrest control back away from the Big Four.

It was Judah's last long journey. Contracting yellow fever while crossing Panama, he died November 2,

Working with pick and shovel, one-horse dump carts and black powder, Central Pacific laborers carved a way through and over the rugged Sierra Nevadas, across 690 miles between Sacramento and Promontory, Utah. Association of American Railroads

Focus on People

THE CHINESE IN CALIFORNIA

In 1855 the *Oriental*, one of two Chinese bilingual newspapers in California, predicted that the west-east route "will be scattered with busy lines of Chinese builders of iron roads, that shall link the two oceans." By 1860 the prediction had come true. Faced with the formidable task of cutting through Sierra Nevada granite, the Central Pacific's big Four at first tried hiring local white miners and gold panners. But these men—more intent on striking it rich than building a railroad—proved undependable working on the line. Still, when Crocker began hiring Chinese workers to do the job, his construction bosses initially balked. As superintendent James Strobridge put it bluntly, "I will not boss Chinese!" Today the precipitous railroad route carved through the Sierras still echoes Crocker's rhetorical reply: "But who said laborers have to be white to build railroads?"

Many of the Chinese who subsequently came to California to build railroads settled to stay in the "Golden State." In addition to the great railroad they helped build, they brought with them another legacy as well—agricultural know-how that serves the state's economy to this day. Their knowledge of drainage techniques, reclamation, irrigation and flood prevention enabled farmers in the great river valleys of the Sacramento and San Joaquin to use nearly 5 million acres of land that had been otherwise unusable. They also imported new crops—including strawberries, sugar beets, celery and asparagus. By 1872 nearly two-thirds of all the vegetables grown in the state were produced by Chinese farmers. With their ability to cut costs and maximize yields, these growers brought economic strength to California agriculture. Many economists credit their influence with saving California from the economic disasters that would hit the rest of the nation in the 1870s and 1890s.

1863, shortly after arriving in New York City. He was not quite 38 years old.

Forgotten for many years, today Theodore Judah's contributions to the transcontinental railroad are recognized in Sacramento's Railroad Museum, while a statue of the pioneer railroad engineer, built 60 years after his death by Southern Pacific employees, stands at the nearby Sacramento Depot.

With Judah out of the picture, the Big Four controlled the building of the Central Pacific. With Stanford in the governor's office, Huntington's job was lobbying in the East for more government funds. Hopkins, a notorious penny-pincher, was elected treasurer, and Crocker was to oversee the actual construction of the line.

Governor Stanford, using a silver spade, had ceremoniously broken ground in Sacramento on January 8, 1863. Not the least of the CP's worries, however, involved the physical difficulties of transporting most of its supplies—including rails, spikes, tools and rolling stock—from East Coast factories to the building

site. Light materials could come across the Isthmus of Panama, but heavier items, such as locomotives, had to come around the South American horn by ship. Even the Panama route added considerable cost to East Coast prices, with rails that sold at $91.70 a ton in the East costing $143.67 on arrival on the West Coast. But on October 7 of that year the Central Pacific's first locomotive, immodestly named the Governor Stanford, arrived in California. By April of 1864 the locomotive was pulling passengers east to Roseville, California and, by June 3, farther east to Newcastle. Most of the ground that it had covered, though, was relatively flat. Now the rugged mountains of the Sierra range loomed ahead.

Crocker's most immediate problem was to find enough track-layers and common laborers to continue the laying of the line. The work was hard, paid poorly and offered few comforts. Besides, the gold rush was still on, and while a man wouldn't *necessarily* get rich prospecting for gold, there was always a *chance* that he could. With prospecting, a man was his own boss, kept his own hours—and could dream

Technology Close-Up

NITROGLYCERIN IN THE SIERRAS

While pickaxes and shovels served well for building a railroad through lowlands, the rocky slopes of the Sierra Nevadas posed a less easily penetrable obstacle. Tons of black powder explosive were imported from the East—powder manufactured in the West was inferior, and only the best had any chance against Sierra granite. When ignited, powder could release gases with explosive force, pushing chunks of material out of the way with its power. But even the best was not powerful enough.

Meanwhile, in 1846, a chemist named Ascanio Sobrero at the Turin Institute of Technology in Italy had discovered he could create a powerful liquid explosive by dripping glycerin slowly into strong sulfuric and nitric acids. The resulting oily yellow liquid could release 12,000 times the volume of gas it contained. Its one drawback was its great instability, with a sensitivity rating of 13 on a scale that designates any rating below 100 as unstable and unsafe.

By the mid-1860s Strobridge recognized the usefulness of this newfangled explosive for blasting tunnels through hard rock. Because nitroglycerin could be inserted in the rock in small holes, drilling time could be cut. And this high explosive's tremendous power could easily shatter the steely granite. To get around the extreme danger of trying to transport it, nitroglycerin was manufactured on the spot at the sites of at least two of the Central Pacific's most challenging tunnels (called Tunnel No. 6 and Tunnel No. 8). The cost was about 75 cents a pound, and building progress increased dramatically—with at least a 50% gain.

of striking it rich enough to buy his own railroad. Those prospects, or even less glamorous enterprises such as farming or storekeeping, looked far better than collecting 75 cents a day, fighting dirt, mountains, brutal line bosses and freezing snow for somebody else. The few men that Crocker did manage to line up usually stayed only long enough to collect a grubstake and then headed out for the gold fields with their friends and dreams. In 1864 the Central Pacific could round up only 1,200 men to work on the railroad. At one point, out of 2,000 workers Crocker hired for one section of track, 1,900 quit and headed for the gold fields before the job was finished.

The situation was so desperate that Crocker tried without success to get the Union Army to give him captured Confederate prisoners. When that ill-conceived idea fell through, he tried to induce Mexican laborers to migrate north, also without success.

His final solution was brilliant though no less controversial. The initial days of the great gold rush had brought many Chinese to California, and although some had struck it rich and returned home, many others had stayed to work as laborers, farmers, house servants for the wealthy and workers in restaurants, laundries and other city jobs. So many had stayed, in

fact, and were still arriving almost daily, that many other Californians began to fear the economic competition. Prejudices ran high, inflamed by derogatory warnings against the influx of the "yellow peril." In fact, Leland Stanford made a political promise that as governor he would restrict Chinese entry into the United States. When Crocker decided as an experiment to hire 50 Chinese laborers to work on the Central Pacific crews, Stanford at first became embarrassed and then did some quick backpedaling.

The "experiment" was a stunning success. Crocker decided to hire more. Then more. After signing up all he could in California, according to some sources, he sent agents to China, recruiting workers on their home soil. What Stanford had to say about this is lost in history, but by the summer of 1866 more than 6,000 Chinese workers were laboring on the Central Pacific rails. Before construction was finished Crocker would employ over 12,000 on the line.

Industrious, inventive and hard-working, the Chinese began pushing the CP roadbed to the mountains and eastward. As one 1865 journal described the scene, "They are laying siege to Nature in her strongest citadel . . . the rugged mountains look like stupendous ant-hills. They swarm with Celestials [Chinese],

A Central Pacific construction camp in Utah, April 1869. Association of American Railroads

season of more than 44 feet. Storm after storm swept in across the Pacific Ocean to break against the Sierra peaks. By the time the tracks had reached a 6,000-foot elevation, each day's work had become an exercise in survival.

To hurry the work, locomotives, cars and rails had been transported over the summit, to the Truckee Valley on the eastern slope, where digging had begun at the same time as workers began tunneling through from the west. A third opening, a vertical shaft from the summit, was completed in December 1866, enabling work to proceed in both directions from the middle as well. Inside, small crews of men chipped at the four faces in the lonely cold, while hundreds of others scratched at six other tunnels in the Sierra face. Occasionally the mountains would shudder with their blasts.

The tunnel work progressed with excruciating slowness. Often no more than a few inches a day could be chipped away from the granite face.

Beneath the heavily crusted snow, Chinese laborers burrowed a labyrinth of tunnels from their half-buried shacks to the mouth of the railroad tunnel, dug air shafts and chimney holes, chiseled stairways of ice and used lanterns for light.

Blizzards raged and avalanches were a constant danger. In one of the winter's worst accidents an

shoveling, wheeling, carting, drilling and blasting rocks and earth . . . " By the end of November 1866, the Central Pacific reached Cisco, a five-hour rail trip over 94 miles of newly laid tracks from Sacramento.

Much as the Irish workers had done on the New York and Erie line, Chinese workers dangled in baskets strung by rope from above to carve a ledge for the roadbed along the sheer cliff faces. There they drilled holes and tamped in powder, scrambling up the lines to safety (usually), as the gunpowder exploded below. Hundreds of others cleared giant redwood trees from the right-of-way. In one area it took a gang of 300 men as much as 10 days to clear a mile for track—felling trees, blasting stumps, ducking chunks of flying wood, routing huge boulders and leveling a path through hillsides of rock.

But now progress stopped dead while workers struggled at the dangerous job of punching a series of tunnels through the unyielding Sierra summit.

Nature challenged the railroaders not only with the formidable mountains, but with one of the worst winters the state had seen in many years. The snow began to fall in October. Hard-packed snow in one valley measured 18 feet, with a total snowfall for the

To speed construction through the Sierras, grading through cuts was started on three or four levels whenever possible so that workers would not interfere with each other. Association of American Railroads

entire camp—men, tents, buildings and machines— was swept away to be buried under the snow at the bottom of a canyon. There were no survivors and the bodies, impossible to recover, had to lay frozen and buried under the snow until spring. Lesser avalanches took other workers, one, two or three at a time.

To make matters worse, the Central Pacific, frustrated at the slow progress, began to use a form of nitroglycerin, a newly developed, highly volatile and dangerous liquid explosive, to blast tunnels through the mountains. The work went faster, but many lives were lost in the erratic explosions. Fortunately the cold weather, which has a tendency to stabilize nitroglycerin and make it less likely to go off by accident, probably prevented many more deaths.

Finally, in late 1867, the CP crews finished the last of some 15 tunnels and dug their way out of the Sierras. For many the "mountain job" had been the worst experience in their lives. One Irish crew boss, writing home to Pennsylvania, called his months at the summit "what Hell would be like if the blasted place really did freeze over." He promised to come

home soon "and take that nice safe and quiet job" in a Philadelphia drugstore.

With the mountains behind them, the Central Pacific crews gained speed as they began to move eastward toward the Nevada desert. It had taken almost 41 months to lay track across the mountains. Now, on the flat lands, Crocker's Chinese crews were heading east at an average of a mile of track a day.

Not all difficulties lay behind, however. As superintendent of construction James H. Strobridge later reported to Leland Stanford, the desert presented difficulties of its own:

In crossing the deserts eastward from the Truckee River, water for men and animals was hauled at one time forty miles. It was necessary to have the heavy work in Palisade Canyon done in advance of the main force, and 3,000 men with 400 horses and carts were sent to that point, a distance of 300 miles in advance of the track. Hay, grain, and all supplies for the men and horses had to be hauled over the desert for that great distance, there being no supplies to be obtained on the entire route. The winter of 1868 and 1869 was

Laying track across the plains of Nevada in 1868. Association of American Railroads

one of severe cold. The construction was in progress in the upper Humboldt Valley, where the ground was frozen to a depth of two to three feet, and material required blasting and treatment like rock which could have been cheaply moved in a more favorable time.

Meanwhile, heading west and moving directly toward them, the other line authorized by Congress, the Union Pacific, had also begun to pick up speed.

Driven not only by rivalry and personal pride, but by the fact that each mile of track meant more money from the government, Crocker pushed his crews harder. When word got to him that the largely Irish crews of the UP had managed to set down over eight miles of track in one day, he sent word back to the Union Pacific that his crews could do better. The Union Pacific's chief engineer, Grenville Dodge, took Crocker's bet and showed up in person to witness the attempt.

Supervised by Strobridge, the Central Pacific crew was well organized and ready. "Our organization was as well drilled as any military company," Strobridge reported later. Starting early in the morning of April 28, 1869, the CP crews went to work. By six o'clock in the evening they had laid 10 miles and 200 feet of track—using more than 3,500 rails with a total weight of over 1,000 tons. The entire job was done, at the crew's own insistence, without a relief team.

"Every bolt was screwed up, every spike driven home," Strobridge reported proudly. And when it was done, "we backed down over that 60 foot of grade at the rate of 25 miles an hour, twelve hundred men riding on the empty flat cars."

It was a momentous achievement, and a record that stands until this day.

In fact, the track-laying was now going so fast, by both the Central Pacific and the Union Pacific, that the two railroads threatened to run out of control and overlap each other. Both, after all, were collecting government funds for each mile of track set in place! Congress acted quickly to stop the redundancy and ordered that both lines would join at a single point and share in driving the final spikes that would connect the nation's first transcontinental railroad line. The meeting point, it was decided, would be Promontory, Utah.

6

BUILDING A RAILROAD ACROSS AMERICA: THE UNION PACIFIC BUILDS WESTWARD 1848–1869

Meanwhile, as the Central Pacific was building eastward across the Sierras, the rival Union Pacific was spinning its track westward from the Mississippi.

Like the route through the granite mountains, the path across the plains had also begun with a survey, the results of which were not nearly so clear-cut as Theodore Judah's vision. After squashing Asa Whitney's proposal, Thomas Hart Benton had commissioned his son-in-law, John C. Frémont, to survey a transcontinental railroad route originating, not surprisingly, in St. Louis. Frémont, famous as "the pathfinder" thanks to his well-publicized western expeditions, packed up his crew and equipment and started west in 1848. This time, however, "the pathfinder" found only disaster and embarrassment, his expedition resulting in total failure. Ten of Frémont's men died along the way and his survey was sketchy at best. Benton nevertheless used the expedition's findings to propose a St. Louis-to-California railroad route.

Benton's wasn't the only proposal, however. By the time Lincoln signed the Pacific Railroad Act in 1862, nearly half a dozen other routes had been surveyed and proposed to Congress. The outbreak of the Civil War effectively eliminated routes that would have originated in the southern states, and the California gold rush eliminated any of the far northern routes that would have terminated north of that state. The logical choice, then, became a middle route, which, beginning at Omaha, Nebraska, more or less followed in the tracks of wagon wheels along the Emigrant Trail, heading west up the Platte River and through southern Wyoming to Utah, Nevada and California.

The route was long and treacherous, winding through unexplored country, mountains, deserts and Indian territory. Fortunately, at the head of the newly formed Union Pacific Railroad were two men eminently qualified for the job: Thomas C. Durant, appointed the line's vice president and general manager, and Grenville M. Dodge, its chief engineer.

Durant, born in Massachusetts in 1820, had been trained as a physician, but after medical school he took a position in an export house and began speculating on the stock market. Quick to spot the future power of transportation, he had become interested in railroads and joined a partnership to build the lines that would become the Michigan Southern, the Chicago and Rock Island, and the Mississippi and Mis-

---

Trains and Dates

PUTTING RAILS ACROSS THE PLAINS
1853–1869

1853   Congress authorizes a survey for the transcontinental railroad route.

1862   The Pacific Railway Act gives the Union Pacific Railroad authority to build westward from Nebraska; the Central Pacific, meanwhile, builds east from California

1863   December. The Union Pacific breaks ground to begin construction. Gauge for the Pacific Railway is set at 4 feet 8½ inches. In 1897 this becomes the standard gauge for the United States.

1864   December. Construction, delayed by financing problems, finally begins on the Union Pacific at Omaha, Nebraska.

1866   May. Grenville Dodge assumes duties as chief engineer for the Union Pacific. Within a year he and the Casement brothers have 10,000 men working on the railroad.

September. More than 180 miles have been completed west of Omaha.

1867   The Union Pacific's financing company, Crédit Mobilier, declares more than 100% dividend to its investors, bringing an outcry against excessively high profits and mishandling of funds.

1868   By the end of the year UP has laid more than 450 miles westward from Omaha.

1869   May 10. The Golden Spike Ceremony at Promontory, Utah celebrates completion of the transcontinental railroad.

---

souri railroads. His surveyor on the Mississippi and Missouri was Grenville Dodge.

When interest in a transcontinental railroad gathered momentum, Durant could see the potential. He hired Dodge to survey possible routes. Meanwhile, he also campaigned for Abraham Lincoln, presidential candidate for the Republican party, which had called for construction of a transcontinental railroad as far back as 1854. With Lincoln in office, Durant then became an active lobbyist for the passage of the Pacific Railroad Act.

Grenville Dodge, born in 1831, had traveled a slightly different path. After receiving a degree in civil and military engineering from Norwich University in 1851, he had headed west to become a surveyor on the Illinois Central Railroad. After completing the line across Iowa, he then surveyed for Durant's Mississippi and Missouri Railroads. At the outbreak of the Civil War he was commissioned as a colonel in the 4th Iowa Infantry. Dodge, who always described himself later as both a soldier and engineer, was of invaluable service to the Union during the war, building new

bridges and rebuilding destroyed or damaged ones. After the war, in 1866 he was elected to Congress, but quit after serving less than a year to go to work with Durant and the newly formed Union Pacific Railroad.

Together Durant and Dodge's backgrounds covered the spectrum of railroad building from financing to engineering; both men also wielded tremendous influence, Durant among political and financial circles and Dodge among the military. During the years of the UP's construction their connections were often called upon.

Just getting construction underway, though, was no easy task. Not having the firsthand financial backing that the Central Pacific was handed by the "Big Four," the Union Pacific spent its fledgling days struggling for funds. And despite the financial incentives offered by the U.S. government, it was more than three years before the line could begin laying track.

The slow start was troublesome enough to prompt Congress to spur both lines. Shortly after the UP finally began laying track, Congress repealed the law forbidding the competing Central Pacific from building more than 150 miles east of the California-Nevada border. The maneuver provided strong incentive to Durant and Dodge's competition, the Big Four, to build fast—because the more miles the CP could lay, the less chance the UP would have to get hold of valuable government land. The building of the transcontinental now had turned into an intense race to see who could lay the most track before the two lines met and completed the railroad link from coast to coast.

For both railroads, the logistics of getting track and supplies to the base camp presented a big problem. On the western end, the Central Pacific had to have most supplies shipped around Cape Horn. Building eastward from Omaha, the Union Pacific had to have its ties and track hauled overland across hundreds of miles of prairie to the eastern bank of the Missouri and then carried across the river by boat—because no bridges as yet existed across the Missouri. Deliveries were slow and expenses were staggering for both railroads. During one particularly rough period, it cost the UP six dollars a tie for each of the literally thousands of railroad ties that had to be hauled to the ever-moving building site.

For its construction crews, the Union Pacific depended mostly on Irish laborers who had immigrated to American to escape the great potato famine. As the Civil War wound to a close, the work crews were increased by veterans seeking work in the stressed economy, or those still psychologically "wound up," looking for new adventures on the westward trek. Whatever reasons had driven them to the railroad, these men were tough and hardened—characteristics they would need to survive in the many trials ahead.

The weather, blistering hot and humid in the summer, turned so cold in the winter that the workers sometimes were forced to burn the railroad's expensive lumber just to survive. Indian attacks were a

Union Pacific workers hover around the paymaster's car. Many were Irish and most were veterans of the Civil War. The average pay was $3 a day. Association of American Railroads

Focus on People

LAYING TRACKS WITH THE CASEMENT BROTHERS

On the Union Pacific the Casement brothers had track-laying down to a science. Their center of operations was a special train that crawled along the tracks as they were being laid. With a locomotive in the back and pushing, the "Casement train" was a well-organized service center. At the front of the train was a flat car loaded with rails. This was usually followed by an office car, sleeping quarters for the track bosses, a carpenter and a machine shop, a kitchen, a telegrapher's car, a "wash-up car," a private dining and sleeping car for the "big bosses," water cars and supply cars. One of the supply cars was reserved for rifles and ammunition in case of Indian attack.

In operation, the Casement train spearheaded a well-oiled assembly line. The train would ease along the newly laid rails just behind a crew of workers who graded and leveled the bed and laid the cross-ties in place. Then on a signal, the 10-man "iron crew," with five for each section of track, would heave the 500- to 700-pound track sections forward and off the car, dropping each section into place on the cross-ties. "Clampers" and "spikers" would then follow and fasten the rails permanently in place. The work was so efficient that the UP crews could lay a mile of track a day, and sometimes two miles or more. And, although the Central Pacific had once accomplished the backbreaking feat of laying over 10 miles in one day, the Casement operation was much faster overall, since its mile-a-day operation moved steadily and regularly day in and day out.

constant danger. And, driven to nervous and physical exhaustion in their race to lay the rails, the hardened workers often became their own worst enemies.

As the tracks slowly crawled west, a caravan of camp followers constantly pursued the workers. Always ready to fleece the men of their earnings, these gamblers, saloonkeepers, dance hall girls, "loan sharks" and rowdies set up shop along the way. Hastily built tent "towns" were erected almost overnight at each new construction point. Some of the towns were elaborate, built not just of tents but of carefully numbered piles of lumber that could be quickly set up and then taken down again only to be reassembled at the next site along the railroad's right-of-way. Each night and each off-shift, the workers poured into these shanty "towns" to drink, gamble, spend their money and enjoy their pleasures.

The "pleasures" weren't always enjoyable, though. The men were often robbed or beaten and occasionally were even killed for whatever they had in their pockets. They were also often too intoxicated to report to work the next morning.

The situation became so intolerable that the Union Pacific decided on drastic measures. It couldn't stop the movement of this "hell on wheels," as the towns were called, but it could nudge them into line a bit.

For this job the UP called on two of its toughest and most respected track bosses, the Casement brothers, Jack and Dan. Expert track-layers who had learned their job during the war and had it down to a science, the brothers also knew how to keep their men in line. If "outsiders" got in the way, then the casement brothers knew how to handle them too.

A typical shanty town. Association of American Railroads

45

Typical of the new railroad "towns," Julesburg, in the Colorado Territory, was one of the toughest of all. In one month it had grown from a town of 40 men and one woman to a town of over 4,000 very transient and rowdy residents. Disturbed by reports of its violence, corruption and flagrant disregard for law and order, Grenville Dodge gave orders to the Casements to help the town's overwhelmed law officers establish order.

The Casement brothers chose a handful of men and moved in. By the time they were finished, Boot Hill (the name given to many transient cemeteries in the Old West) was overflowing, and the town was nearly deserted. Buildings, tents and quick-buck artists all had departed to easier and safer money elsewhere.

The Great American Desert, as the region was aptly called, held other threats not so easily met, however. Gamblers, hucksters and gunfighters might be contained, if not stopped, but Indians were another matter altogether, even for men like the tough-minded

Casement brothers. The Union Pacific's route called for laying track across the great open plains of Nebraska and Wyoming, directly through Indian country. While farther west the Central Pacific had solved its "Indian problems" by offering passes and free rides to the relatively peaceful Digger and Snake tribes, the UP was faced with the fierce and proud Sioux. Dodge's military contacts came in handy and the railroad was given army protection as it crawled slowly across the hills and plains, but there simply wasn't enough army to go around. "You can't surround three Indians with one soldier," one army officer wrote to his superiors in exasperation.

Fighting against the intrusion on their homeland, and fearing that the "iron horse" and white men would steal their land and destroy their way of life, the Sioux were relentless in their resistance, attacking, skirmishing and counterattacking at every opportunity. The white man's indiscriminate slaughter of buffalo not just for food but for hides and sport added more fuel to the Indians' anger. The Indians

Though Indians and climate presented many obstacles, the work continued. This photo shows the end of the Union Pacific Track near Archer, Wyoming in 1867. Association of American Railroads

Life on the Railroad

THE END OF THE LINE

After the completion of the transcontinental railroad, most of the principal figures in its construction moved on to other projects. The Central Pacific's "Big Four" continued to expand their personal empires. Charles Crocker became president of the Southern Pacific Railroad and personally supervised much of the building. In combination with the Union Pacific, the Southern Pacific quickly became a major force in the economic and political life of the American Far West.

Crocker's fortune continued to grow, and by the time of his death he was one of the wealthiest men in California. In 1866, however, he was severely injured in a carriage accident while visiting New York City. His health never returned and he died in Monterey, California in 1888.

Collis Huntington continued to expand his personal fortune through the Union Pacific and Southern Pacific lines. Always a "money-man" at heart, he spent his last years attempting to find loopholes in the loan agreements that the railroads had made with the government.

Leland Stanford, who had never really been an effective politician except in matters involving the railroad, downplayed his interest in politics and continued his railroad investing. Elected to the United States Senate in 1884, his years of service were undistinguished and he was often accused of missing important votes and paying little attention to nonrailroad matters. In 1885 he endowed Leland Stanford Junior University in honor of his son, who had died at the age of 15. The university, now known simply as Stanford, became one of the best endowed and most highly respected universities in the country. Stanford Senior died in 1893.

Mark Hopkins, who, with Stanford, had attended the ceremonies at Promontory, died in his private railroad car in Yuma, Arizona in 1878. He was inspecting the Southern Pacific's progress into the Southwest. At the time of his death, his fortune was valued at $25 million. Today one of San Francisco's major hotels bears his name.

Thomas C. Durant, who had amassed a great deal of money through his financial manipulations while building the Union Pacific, had also amassed a great many enemies, some of whom were on the company's board of directors. Two weeks after the Golden Spike ceremony Durant was voted off the board. His health failed shortly afterward and he retired a wealthy man to a mansion in the Adirondack Mountains. He was planning a railroad from the Adirondacks into Canada at the time of his death in 1885.

Grenville Dodge continued on the Union Pacific until 1871 and then went to work for the Texas and Pacific Railroad. When that line failed, he continued working for various railroads throughout the Southwest until his death in 1916.

The Casement brothers continued working on the Union Pacific and eventually faded from history.

ambushed survey parties, scalped telegraph repair crewmen, blockaded tracks, shot bodies full of arrows and roasted men alive. Hatred flamed on both sides, with General William Sherman at one point writing with little compassion, "The more we can kill this year, the less will have to be killed in the next war, for the more I see of these Indians the more convinced I am that they all have to be killed or maintained as a species of paupers."

The Cheyenne joined in the attacks, demonstrating their contempt for the hopelessly outnumbered military by openly riding into Cheyenne, Wyoming during a Fourth of July celebration in 1867, where they attacked and killed several of the celebrants. Late that same summer a Cheyenne war party succeeded in derailing a Union Pacific handcar and smashing a train that was headed down the track near Plum Creek. As Porcupine, a young Cheyenne brave who witnessed the wreck, explained, the attack followed a

The meeting of two great railroads at Promontory, Utah on May 10, 1869. Amid great ceremony, the last spike, made of gold, was driven to join the rails from east and west, and the celebration began. Association of American Railroads

fight between soldiers and a group of Cheyenne and Sioux that had left the Indians defeated and destitute. "We were feeling angry," he explained simply, continuing his account:

> Not long after that we saw the first train of cars that any of us had seen. We looked at it from a high ridge. Far off it was very small, but it kept coming and growing larger all the time, puffing out smoke and steam, and as it came on we said to each other that it looked like a white man's pipe when he was smoking.

From the wreckage and death of that day, the Indians emerged jubilant and victorious. But the white man's pipe continued to smoke as the Union Pacific pushed relentlessly on.

With his hands full on the frontier, the Union Pacific's chief engineer was also having trouble with the home office. In what was becoming a sad refrain in the histories of the early railroads, greed and corruption had infected management. Complicated back-room maneuvering was draining funds from the line and putting it

in the pockets of a small group of influential board members and stockholders. In one instance Dodge, who was proud of his engineering skill and wanted to build the line to be as economical and functional as possible, found himself in conflict with Durant and others in management who were trying to stretch the line along less direct routes so they could collect more money from the government. Dodge won this skirmish, at least, when General Ulysses S. Grant, called in to settle the dispute, sided with him.

Finally, in the early months of 1869, the Union Pacific crossed the Utah border and was nearing Promontory. By this time Congress had designated this point for the historic meeting of both ends of the transcontinental railroad.

Feelings were running high. The "race" had been a hard one, and the two railroads had little love for one another. As the lines approached each other, trouble began to break out between the two crews. Small acts of maliciousness and vandalism escalated into larger, more violent attacks, and a number of workers on both lines were killed.

The long race was just about over, however, by May of 1869 when Promontory came into view.

THE GOLDEN SPIKE

On May 10, 1869 the small "shanty town" of Promontory, Utah found itself overflowing with crowds of celebrating, high-toned visitors. The dusty streets were a jumble of excitement and confusion. Well-dressed dignitaries and politicians mixed with not-so-well-dressed journalists, gaudy dance-hall girls and sweat-stained miners, mule drivers and railroad workers. Most of the politicians and dignitaries remained sober, at least until the picture taking was over—an admirable achievement in the throat-parching dust.

The gathered press, however, worried less about public opinion. They shared bottles with the railroad workers, lighted free cigars and scribbled notes while waiting for the historic moment that would soon take place.

In the center of all this boisterous activity two hulking locomotives—the Jupiter, representing the Central Pacific, and No. 119, representing the Union Pacific—stood a few yards apart waiting to touch their cowcatchers together as the tracks of the two railroad lines were about to meet. The excitement stretched beyond Promontory. All over the nation milling crowds waited near telegraph stations to be the first to hear the news. On the East and West coasts bell-ringers in churches, school houses and fire departments prepared to sound the news that the first coast-to-coast railroad had been completed. A special telegraph line had even been attached to the final spike so that the exact moment could be captured.

Standing near the tracks in stony dignity, Governor Leland Stanford prepared to help hammer in the last spike for the Central Pacific. Alongside him, Dr. Thomas Durant would take his swing for the Union Pacific. The final spike, symbolically, was gold.

Although the historic event certainly had enough witnesses, there is some confusion about what happened next. The governor apparently swung—and missed the spike. And Durant, trying his hand, missed it too! Who actually drove in the final spike is lost to history, although the most reliable accounts of the day say that UP Chief Engineer Grenville Dodge finally finished the job.

Whatever the truth of the story, the transcontinental railroad was complete. The two locomotives edged toward each other. The cowcatchers touched. Bells

pealed out. People all over the nation shook hands, hugged and danced in the streets.

In Promontory, more bottles were broken out and more photographs taken. Later Stanford, not liking the somewhat boisterous atmosphere that the camera saw, commissioned his own painting of the occasion. More dignified and sedate, Stanford's own version also included his partners, who actually weren't even in Promontory at the time.

It didn't really matter though. For the Irish and Chinese crews who had built it, and the construction bosses and engineers who had seen it through, the real story of the transcontinental railroad had already taken place. Their labor had forever changed the face of America.

The Union Pacific and the Central Pacific had accomplished what many had considered the impossible, building across "an uninhabitable country," as described by railroad engineer Henry Varnum Poor in 1854, " . . . over mountain ranges whose summits are white with eternal snows; over deserts parched beneath an unclouded sky, and over yawning chasms. . . ."

Within a week a fully loaded freight train from Chicago was heading west. And a new era in American history had begun.

In 1857 Theodore Judah had prophesied:

> And be it remembered that it is not the through lines to California alone upon which the road is to rely for through travel. There is Utah, Oregon, Washington, the Russian possessions, the Sandwich Islands [now Hawaii], China and the Far East Indies—all of which are brought, more or less within the influence of the road.

John C. Frémont had seen the possibilities too, writing enthusiastically: "America will be between Asia and Europe—the golden vein which runs through the history of the world will follow the track to San Francisco. . . ."

With the final spike driven in 1869, today's much-touted "Pacific Rim" market, vital to the economics of the 1990s, was born. What had once been a nation cut in two by an uncrossable desert—vast, parched and barren—now was a nation joined by ribbons of rail.

While the national economy did suffer untold losses due to what one economic historian calls "fast-and-loose rail financing," as prevalent on the CP and UP lines as elsewhere, it also gained immeasurably from the completed network. Now the gold and silver fields of the Rocky Mountains were accessible. Surges of population swelled the area, with thousands forming service communities of innkeepers, storekeepers, farmers, saloonkeepers and blacksmiths. And by 1880 the Mountain State region had the second highest per-capita income in the nation. Much of that wealth was thanks to the railroad across American built by the Central Pacific and the Union Pacific. And thanks to others that would follow, to the north and south, with a rapidly growing trail of networks into the West.

Railroads in 1870. With the first transcontinental railroad completed, railroads also had begun to network through the Mississippi and Missouri River valleys. Even though construction was halted during the Civil War, more than 22,000 miles of track were laid between 1860 and 1870. Association of American Railroads

7

HEYDAY OF THE RAILROADS
1870–1914

With the transcontinental railroad completed, East Coast America finally had its link with the West. Meanwhile, as the Union Pacific and Central Pacific were chiseling, blasting and pounding their way across the miles, railroads had also been progressing on other fronts. In the same month that Lincoln signed the act authorizing the railroad's westward route, the first experimental car designed for sorting mail en route went into service between Hannibal and St. Joseph, Missouri. The first permanent mail car went into service two years later, in 1864, between Chicago and Clinton, Iowa. Passenger comfort was also improving. In 1863 the first dining cars were introduced on the heavily traveled run between Philadelphia and Baltimore. And in 1868 the luxurious Delmonico, the first dining car built by George Pullman, was put into service.

Operational systems had also been quietly improving. In 1863 the first "block-signal" system was introduced—making rail traffic safer and more efficient. The system divided track into sections, or blocks, with signals positioned at the beginning of each section. The sections were spaced so that trains would always be traveling a safe distance from each other. Movable signal arms could be set in semaphore positions to inform the engineer about conditions on the track ahead. If another train was ahead, depending on its distance, a "Caution" signal could be displayed, or a

"Stop." (Today these signals, which are often colored lights, are activated electrically when the train's wheels cross into the block.)

The first "tank car" took to the rails in 1865. Privately owned, it was used to transport oil from Titusville, Pennsylvania, the site of the first American oil well. The railroad soon replaced the tank wagons and flatboats that had been used to haul crude oil to the refineries, although at first the railroads insisted that shippers supply their own tank cars. In the 1870s and 1880s, however, oil industrialist John D. Rockefeller discovered that by gaining control of 90% of the tank car fleet, he could control a large share of the nation's lucrative petroleum industry—which was rapidly gaining key importance in the industrial economy. By 1878 multimillionaire Rockefeller dominated the country's oil industry.

The automatic coupler, invented by Eli Hamilton Janney in 1868 and patented in 1873, would also make life easier and safer for brakemen and yard workers. Until Janney came up with his invention, the most common coupler was a pin-and-link arrangement that required brakemen to go between the cars and couple and uncouple them by hand. So many brakemen had lost fingers, hands, legs and lives that railway safety crusader Lorenzo Coffin observed, "I discovered it was taken as a *matter of course* that railroad men of necessity be maimed and killed." The Janney coupler worked

Life on the Railroad

THE GREAT TRAIN ROBBERS

The first recorded train robbery in history occurred on May 5, 1865 when a gang of unknown men held up an Ohio and Mississippi train running between St. Louis, Missouri and Cincinnati, Ohio. The robbers were never caught. The idea, however, did catch on.

Sam Bass, Jesse and Frank James, the Dalton Brothers, the Younger Brothers, the Reno Brothers, Butch Cassidy and the Sundance Kid, and dozens of other less famous bad men soon took up the activity.

Although the prime targets for the bandits were trains running through the then "wild western" states of Kansas and Missouri, during its brief heyday train robbing reached just about anywhere a railroad laid its tracks. Operating mostly in groups (made up preferably of brothers or close, "trusted" relatives), the outlaws hit trains from California to New Mexico to Illinois. Obviously, a group effort worked best when attacking a train well packed with passengers and railroad personnel, but a few intrepid bandits liked to work solo. The preferred method of operation in that case was to hit a short train, or to stow aboard a longer one and stick up a single passenger car or freight car before making a quick exit. A brief "fad" found the solo bandit hiding in a box or coffin and shipping himself down the line, interrupting his journey long enough to pop out of his hiding place, stick up the freight car and jump out the door—with any luck at the right place where he had left a horse waiting.

The gangs were for the most part noisier and more dangerous. Caught up in their own exuberance and the power of their six-guns, they were wild west terrorists, forcing obedience by indiscriminately shooting at the train, passengers, train crew and just about whatever else took their fancy. Despite this, some, like the James brothers, became folk heroes who, according to popular mythology, robbed the cruel railroad barons and gave money to poor farmers. Most of the money and valuables traveling aboard the trains, of course, belonged to somebody other than the hated railroad magnates, and there is no evidence that the James boys ever turned their booty over to starving farmers. But America, like most other countries in the world, had a soft spot in its heart for "Robin Hood" legends.

The famous Pinkerton Detective Agency and concentrated activities by law enforcement officers get credit for ending the brief period of great train robberies. But in fact, the arrival of faster and larger locomotives eventually made the whole job if not impossible, simply more work and danger than most bandits cared to put up with.

like two hands clasping vertically, with fingers bent at the knuckles. Brakemen could control coupling and uncoupling by a lever without walking between the cars—providing an enormous improvement in safety. By 1877 the McConway & Torley Corporation began using Janney's automatic coupler on passenger cars, and after extensive testing, the Master Car Builders Association officially adopted the coupler.

Many brakemen also lost their balance—and their lives—turning the old-style hand brakes commonly used on freight trains in the 19th century. Upstate New Yorker George Westinghouse's invention, the air brake, patented in 1869, promised to solve the prob-

lem. But at first few railroads adopted it—perhaps, as clergyman-journalist Lyman Abbott accused, because "brakes cost more than trainmen." Finally, in a test conducted by the Master Car Builders Association, Westinghouse's brake brought a Chicago, Burlington and Quincy freight train to a hissing stop within 500 feet. Widespread replacement of the old, hand-turned brake soon began, and the Railroad Safety Appliance Act of 1893 made both air brake and automatic coupler required by law.

Meanwhile, all across the nation more track was being planned and laid, much of it in the midwestern and western portions of the United States.

Brakemen connecting railroad cars with the old link-and-pin couplers often lost fingers, limbs and even their lives. Association of American Railroads

THE ATCHISON, TOPEKA AND SANTA FE

It took more than a little imagination to see Kansas as a peaceful land of opportunity in the mid-1850s. Today's sprawling symbol of the fertile and peaceful Midwest was in those days a rowdy and untamed frontier. Deserving of its nickname, "Bloody Kansas" was a "wild west" land of cowtowns and cowboys, gunfights and gunfighters, drifters and schemers.

Despite the harsh reality, though, even before the Civil War a man named Cyrus K. Holliday had envisioned a different kind of Kansas and had dreamed of building a railroad through the state. His dream was not just for the railroad but for Kansas and its people, for a time when the land and the towns would be tamed and farmers with hoes and seed would replace the cowboys, guns and bullets. In the meantime, though, the cowtowns and trail herds would make valuable revenue for the fledgling railroad.

A lawyer with a quick mind and an eloquent speaking style, Holliday joined in the territory's politics and helped lay out what was to be the state capital of Topeka. When Kansas was admitted to the Union in 1861, Holliday was a featured speaker at its constitutional convention.

In 1859 he had managed to get a charter to begin building his dream—the Atchison and Topeka Rail-

road. But, as others before him had learned, a charter wasn't necessarily a railroad. And not until 1863, when Congress, eager to keep Kansas in the Union, authorized land grants to the line, was Holliday able to secure enough funds to begin construction.

By then Holliday's dream had stretched out to include Santa Fe, New Mexico, an active and growing center of produce and trade. The route would be along the heavily traveled Santa Fe Trail. Now, instead of wagon ruts, fresh, shining track would speed people and goods across Kansas to New Mexico.

The railroad's agreement with the government called for the Atchison, Topeka and Santa Fe (also known simply as the Santa Fe) to extend to the Colorado border within 10 years. Then it could lay claim to the land the government had promised. Holliday began laying his track in the fall of 1868.

Like the Union Pacific, the AT&SF found itself creating boom towns that sprang up along its right-of-

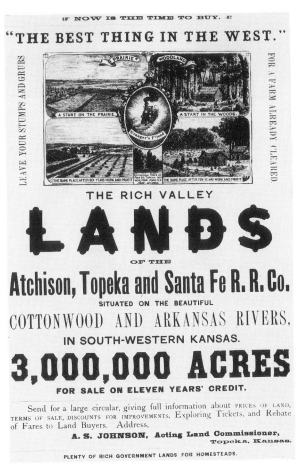

This AT&SF poster enticed potential buyers by promoting the advantages of prairie farming, as opposed to woodland farming in other parts of the country. Association of American Railroads

During the hostilities of 1878–79, these Denver & Rio Grande riflemen marked out a "dead line" for Santa Fe tracklayers in the Royal Gorge: "Thus far could they come, and no further." Denver Public Library

way. By 1871 the AT&SF had reached the infamous Dodge City, a cowtown so tough that, lacking enough lumber to enlarge its jails, it simply dug a wide, 15-foot-deep hole in the ground and dumped its lawbreaking citizens inside to cool off. Because a strong animosity had sprung up between the tough railroad workers and the hard-driving and hard-drinking cowboys, the passage through Dodge City and other cow towns was a rough one, and both sides lost many men through fistfights and gunfights along the way.

By 1872, a bit ahead of schedule, the tracks reached the Colorado border and the AT&SF claimed its needed land grants—alternate sections ten miles wide on either side of its right-of-way—nearly three million acres in all. With new funds coming in, the line continued to push westward. Knowing that the railroad would need enough people and goods to make a profit, the AT&SF began offering its land for sale to anyone who would settle there. Posters and recruiting agents spread north, south, east and west promoting Kansas land and encouraging immigrants. The railroad even sent its agents to Europe and Russia to recruit farmers and settlers to move into the area along the AT&SF's right-of-way.

It was a brilliant move, and homesteaders and settlers poured in. The late 1870s would bring devastating droughts and plagues of grasshoppers so thick that the railroad wheels couldn't get enough traction to move over their squashed bodies—but the state of Kansas fought and prospered and so did the AT&SF.

BATTLE SCENES IN THE CANYONS OF THE COLORADO

Meanwhile, though, another railroad man was beginning to make his dream a reality. William Jackson Palmer was a tough ex-Civil War general who had first become involved with the railroads at the age of 18 when he began surveying for a small Pennsylvania short line. After the war he had become chief of construction for the Kansas Pacific Railroad and had ventured into mining and real estate.

In 1870 Palmer founded the Denver and Rio Grande, a railroad line that would stretch from Colorado to the Mexican border to serve the rich silver mining interests. Palmer's route was a tough one, dismaying many experienced railroad men. The line would have to cross the heart of the Rocky Mountains, navigating high peaks and deep canyons while crossing and recrossing the Great Divide. To make matters worse, the line had to pass through the Royal Gorge of the Arkansas River and over the high Raton Pass in New Mexico. Unfortunately, the Atchison, Topeka & Santa Fe was also intending to use Raton Pass in its journey over the mountains at the Colorado border and down into Santa Fe.

By 1878, as track from both railroads continued to approach the pass, a showdown appeared inevitable. Under new management, the AT&SF had hired William Barstow Strong in December 1877 as its general manager. A tough veteran of railroad building, Strong had worked his way up through the ranks and was able and experienced in handling trouble. And the Denver and Rio Grande was going to be trouble. Strong's first move, though, was not against that railroad but against the Southern Pacific. The SP had originally been founded in 1865 to build a line from San Francisco to San Diego, California. It had been taken over by the Central Pacific's Big Four in 1868 in their drive to expand their rail network through the far western states. By this time the SP had extended eastward from California as far as the Arizona–New Mexico border and was about to enter New Mexico. Regarding the territory as their own, the Big Four were now trying to keep both the AT&SF *and* the Denver and Rio Grande out of New Mexico. But Strong disposed of the Southern Pacific's somewhat weak legal arguments with some fancy legal maneuvering of his own, and then turned his attention to the Denver and Rio Grande.

His strategy was simple: Get to the pass first and hold it by force if necessary. He ordered his workmen to keep building. Then he rounded up a gang of heavily armed men and headed for the pass himself. The Denver and Rio Grande had decided on the same strategy. They were just a little slower. By the time the D&RG crews arrived, the Santa Fe was already there, well armed and waiting.

The situation, though explosive, never erupted into violence. The Denver and Rio Grande backed away from the confrontation. Tempers flared briefly but, almost miraculously, not a shot was fired and the Santa Fe began laying its track the next day.

Strong had won his first battle with the Denver and Rio Grande. But it wouldn't be his last. With both railroads building in the same territory, another clash was inevitable. The next confrontation occurred at the Royal Gorge of the Arkansas River, a narrow 3,000-foot-deep rift in the Rocky Mountains, just west of Pueblo. Both railroads had their eyes on the canyon as a way to get track through to the profitable Colorado mining country around Leadville.

This time there was bloodshed.

While lawyers for both sides battled in the courts, once again the crews armed and prepared for action. Gunfire broke out up and down both lines. Still smarting from their humiliation at Raton Pass, the Denver and Rio Grande crews packed a train with over 200 armed men and terrorized the Santa Fe's supply stations and depots. Santa Fe agents and their families were beaten and kidnapped as the train moved from station to station. In Cuchara, two Santa Fe men were killed and two others seriously wounded. Engaging in sniping tactics of their own, the Santa Fe men attacked and beat D&RG workers and supporters. In one of the more dramatic showdowns between the two railroads, the Santa Fe hired gunfighter, and sometime law officer, Bat Masterson to protect its station at Pueblo. Masterson moved in with a gang of hand-picked gunmen and waited for the D&RG raiders to arrive. Confronted by the notorious Masterson and his accomplices, the Denver and Rio Grande crew did the smart thing. They quickly dropped their rifles and pulled out their money bags, buying Masterson and his men off.

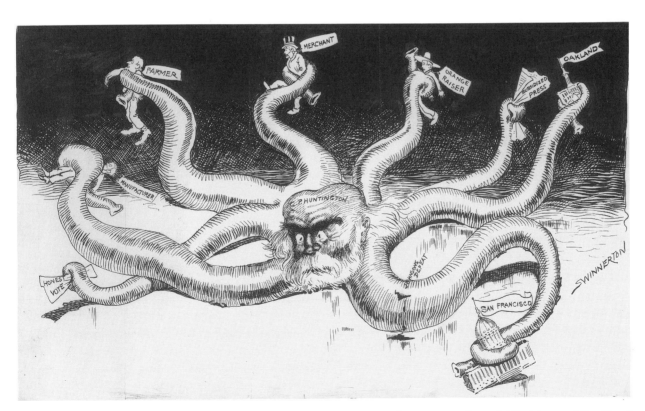

C. P. Huntington as octopus, choking the honest vote, manufacturer, farmer, merchant, orange raiser, subsidized press and the cities of Oakland and San Francisco in its tentacles. Originally published in the San Francisco Examiner *in 1896. California State Library*

Life on the Railroad

THE SLEEPING CAR

Designs for sleeping cars go back at least as far as 1829, when R. F. Morgan of Stockbridge, Massachusetts built a double-decker car with an awning-covered promenade on the upper deck and five berths, or beds, on the deck below. Others followed with various designs, many of them ingenious. A passenger riding aboard the New York Central in 1860 described the sleeping car he traveled in as an ordinary railroad coach—that is, until the officer of the sleeping car began to transform it for the night:

> . . . with trim neatness and quick hand the nimble Yankee turns over every other seat, so as to reverse the back, and make two seats, one facing the other. . . . Smartly he strips up the cushions and unfastens from beneath each seat a can-bottomed frame, there secreted. In a moment, opening certain ratchet holes in the wall of the carriage, he has slided these in at a proper height above, and covered each with cushions and sleeping rug.
> I go outside on the balcony, to be out of the way, and when I come back the whole place is transformed. No longer an aisle of double seats; like a section of a proprietary chapel put snug for sleeping, with curtained berths and closed portholes.

George Pullman, of course, is the man whose name became synonymous with the sleeping car. His first ran from Bloomington, Illinois to Chicago in September 1858 and already boasted his most original innovation, the upper berth that tucked away out of sight, while neatly storing the bedding by day. In this first model, the upper berth pulled down from the ceiling on pulleys and attached to vertical iron rods. But by 1864 Pullman had invented and patented his hinged upper berth that folded out of sight against the side of the car. At the same time he patented a hinged design for the seats, which faced each other and slid down so the back lay flat and the two seats slid forward to touch in the middle, forming the lower berth. This was the model he offered to Mrs. Lincoln as she accompanied President Lincoln's body aboard the funeral train in 1865. His first sleeping car, the Pioneer, cost $20,000 to build and was wider than standard passenger cars. To let the funeral train pass, with the Pullman car attached, the Alton and Chicago Railroad had to modify several of its stations along the way.

In 1867 Pullman went on to develop what he called a Hotel Car, a combined sleeping and dining car. His first dining car, the Delmonico, went into use in 1868, and in 1870 he put together the first coast-to-coast train to travel from Boston to San Francisco with no change of cars required.

The battles in the canyons and the courtrooms seesawed back and forth for months, but in the end the lawyers won the war. The courts awarded the right-of-way to the Denver and Rio Grande. Exhausted and losing money and time by their long fight, the Santa Fe continued to resist for a few weeks, but in the end signed a peace agreement in February of 1880. The D&RG got control of the valuable Colorado mining territory and the Santa Fe was allowed to continue on to its destination of Santa Fe, New Mexico.

THE BIG FOUR EMPIRE CONTINUES TO EXPAND

While the Denver and Rio Grande scrapped with the Santa Fe over routes in New Mexico and Colorado, another giant line was building its own connections. Even before the Central Pacific finished its track in the transcontinental link the Big Four had begun to make plans for extending their holdings throughout the west, and adding the SP line was only part of the plan.

Trains and Dates
1869–1914

1869	George Westinghouse patents the air brake.
1870	First coast-to-coast through train runs from Boston to San Francisco.
1873	First north-south through train between Chicago and New Orleans. A ferry is used to cross the Ohio river and a car change is required at Cairo, Illinois, due to a change in track gauge.
1875	First Pullman parlor car is put into service.
1876	July 1. Official opening of the Great Hoosac Tunnel in western Massachusetts.
1880	Alonzo C. Mather invents the first humane stock car.
1881	First tests of telephone communication on the railroads at Altoona, Pennsylvania.
	First steam heating system installed in a passenger train.
1883	January. Direct rail route is completed from California to New Orleans (Southern Pacific).
	First rail route is completed connecting Washington territory to the Great Lakes (the Northern Pacific).
1884	Through traffic is opened from Chicago to the Pacific Northwest (Huntington, Oregon) via a middle transcontinental route (via the Oregon Short Line).
1885	The automatic coupler, invented by Janney, is approved by Master Car Builders Association.
1887	The rail route from the Great Lakes is extended through the Cascade Mountains to Puget Sound (Northern Pacific).
	Interstate Commerce Act creates the Interstate Commerce Commission (ICC).
	On New York-to-Chicago run, solidly built vestibules between passenger cars are used for the first time.
	The north-south direct route line is completed on the West Coast between Seattle, Washington, Portland, Oregon, San Francisco and Los Angeles (Southern Pacific).
1888	One million freight cars are in service in the United States.
1893	Federal law requires air brakes and automatic couplers.
1894	Strikes among railroad workers in the Midwest freeze transportation along 50,000 miles of railroad lines.
1897	The Supreme Court rules that 18 railroads are in violation of the Sherman Antitrust Act in associating to set transportation rates.
1899	Locomotive No. 999 makes the first 100-mph run.
1900	April 30. Engineer Casey Jones dies. A ballad telling his tale appears first in sheet music two years later.
1901	First mechanical coal-stokers are introduced for locomotives.
1902	More than 200,000 miles of railroad track stretch across the United States.
1905	The Broadway Limited of the Pennsylvania Railroad makes the fastest passenger run yet, at 127.06 miles per hour.
1906	Passage of the Railroad Rate Bill gives the federal government the right to set rates for interstate commerce.
1910	Pennsylvania Station, the New York City terminal of the Pennsylvania Railroad, opens and with it service through tunnels under the Hudson and East rivers.
1914	First tests are made using radio for railroad communications.

While many eastern speculators built their railroads for the profits they could wring out of them before selling out, the Big Four intended to build a railroad empire that was permanent and self-sustaining.

With the Southern Pacific in their control, stretching south from San Francisco to San Diego, and the Central Pacific connecting the transcontinental link, they quickly began to buy up or build a network of spurs and short lines. With the Yuba Railroad they sent a line of track from Sacramento into northern California. In the opposite direction they built a CP spur south from Sacramento and into the fertile farmland of the San Joaquin Valley. By buying up other short lines or forcing them out of business, the SP, by 1884, owned every mile of standard-gauge railroad track in the State of California.

Through the years its network of rails grew longer and more intricate. Each year new track owned by the Big Four spread across the state and then into the rest of the west from Texas to Oregon. The SP itself stretched from San Francisco to Los Angeles, and east across southern Arizona, New Mexico and Texas until by 1883 it reached all the way to New Orleans.

The CP/SP network of rails would not only make the Big Four wealthier, it would make California one of the richest and most productive states in the Union. Later, known simply as the SP, the Southern Pacific would dominate California politics for years, becoming for some a symbol of the state's economic wealth and growth and for others a hated, many-armed monster, an "octopus" thriving on graft and corruption.

Whatever it was, savior or sinner, there was no stopping it. The Age of the Railroad had arrived in the West, and the SP, tying together farms, mines, cities, ports and industries, helped to change the nation's balance of economy. As one SP brochure put it: "SP helped develop the West, and the West in turn helped develop SP. S's history is, in fact, impossible to separate from the pageant of America's westward migration in the 19th and 20th centuries."

OUT OF CONTROL: A TIME FOR REFORM

The SP was not alone in its conquest of the West. By the early 1880s the entire face of the "wild west" was changing as networks of rails snaked out across mountains, deserts and prairies. The Missouri-Kansas-Texas Railroad, known simply as the "Katy," stretched from Kansas into Texas along old cattle trails. The Kansas Pacific pushed into Denver, while the Denver Pacific headed north to tie into the Union Pacific at Cheyenne, Wyoming. Crossing Colorado, the Denver and Rio Grande tapped the rich mining country, while farther south the Texas and Pacific moved west to El Paso and the AT&SF continued southward to Albuquerque. Dozens of other short lines joined the western track-laying rush.

Interior views of early railroad cars, reproduced from a Chicago, Burlington & Quincy timetable of the 1880s. Note the seats made into beds in the Pullman sleeper on the right. The upper berths (just visible behind the drapes) usually folded down from the wall of the car. Association of American Railroads

As the railroads spread across the West and Midwest, the lines to the north, south and east also continued to grow and consolidate. From 36,000 miles of track at the end of the Civil War, U.S. railroads had leaped to 93,000 miles by the early 1880s and to over 164,000 miles by the end of the decade.

Locomotives, railroad cars, tracks and service had also taken giant leaps forward. The locomotives had become larger, more fuel efficient and powerful; the cars, larger and more specialized for handling different cargo duties; the tracks, stronger and more standardized in gauge; and the service faster, more comfortable and reliable.

America was now a nation of rails. And, thanks in large measure to the railroad, it had been transformed into a land of tremendous wealth and vitality. The railroad not only allowed the nation to move and sell its goods at a tremendous rate, it also created major industries of its own. Besides the hundreds of thousands of workers it employed, it also indirectly employed many others who serviced or supplied it. Not only did it carry coal; it bought it and burned it at a stupendous rate. Iron and steel industries thrived as they quickly turned out more and more rail for the ever-growing lines.

The railroads also helped create a new class of consumer items. Specialty goods and luxuries, once limited to small local markets, now could be moved almost anywhere in the states, creating almost instant fads and trends.

And the railroads encouraged innovation and inventiveness. New products and technologies could be introduced and sold on a wide scale, allowing new businesses and industries to thrive and prosper. Conversely, as the nation became wealthy, so did the railroads.

Some Americans, though, were beginning to think that the railroads were becoming too wealthy. And much too powerful. Much had changed since the pioneering days when men like John Stevens struggled to get enough money to build their railroad lines. By the mid- and late-1800s railroads were big business. And, while many honest and sincere men were drawn into the business and its potential for legitimate profit, other less honest and less sincere ones saw the fast-growing railroad industry as an opportunity to line their pockets with gold.

By the late 1800s a long history of scandal and corruption had begun to shake the public's confidence in the honesty of the railroads. During the 1860s one of the most profitable railroads in the East, the Lake Erie and Western Railroad—originally the New York and Erie and popularly known just as "The Erie"—had fallen into the hands of a seedy band of stock manipulators and confidence men. By the time this group, headed by the notorious Jay Gould, was finished, not only was the Erie plundered of funds but the stock market itself plunged into financial crisis.

Scandals had also tarnished the glory of the first transcontinental railroad when the back-room dealing and money and stock manipulation of the Union Pacific made headlines shortly after the line's completion.

With little government control over their actions and enjoying a virtual monopoly in transportation, the railroads had become, in the eyes of many, much too powerful and self-serving. Sadly, in many cases the public's perception was true. Caught up in increasing competition among themselves and spurred by the lure of tremendous profits, by the late 1800s many American railroads had adopted a public-be-damned policy. Incontestable rate hikes, favoritism to "special customers," open bribery of public officials, "land grabbing" for desired rights-of-way and occasional violence against protesters fueled the public's distrust and hatred.

Particularly vulnerable to unfair and corrupt railroad practices were the nation's many small farmers who depended on the railroads to move their crops and produce. Unable to find satisfaction in the courts, in 1867 a group of western farmers organized the National Grange of the Patrons of Husbandry. By 1875 the organization had grown to over 800,000 members. The first effective organization to challenge the railroad's power, "The Grange" managed to get many state legislatures to pass laws regulating the railroads' freight rates and practices. When the Supreme Court ruled in 1886 that the states could not pass laws regulating goods that crossed over state lines, enough attention had been drawn to the problem that the U.S. Congress established the Interstate Commerce Act, which in 1887 gave the U.S. government some regulatory powers.

The railroad's power was also challenged by its own employees. Beset by dangerous and difficult working conditions, below-standard wages, and the high-handed and indifferent attitude of management, many railroad workers had formed or joined unions. Strikes and violence broke out in many eastern cities. The railroads fought back with increasing violence of their own, employing "strikebreakers," local police forces and state militia. Hundreds of workers were beaten, maimed or killed. In one of the most violent and notorious confrontations, the strike against the Pullman Company in 1894, federal troops were called in and over two dozen strikers were shot down in the streets.

Overall, the period from 1870 to 1914 saw many technical advances that made railroads safer, more comfortable for passengers and more efficient and versatile for the movement of freight. New routes in the West, such as the Atchison, Topeka & Santa Fe and the Denver & Rio Grande—along with the considerable expansion and growth of the powerful Southern Pacific—established new links among midwestern, mountain and southwestern regions. It was a time when railroads made a great contribution to the country's growing economy, but also a time when greed, corruption and graft among railroad financiers, builders and owners created considerable scandal and financial loss.

During this same period two more great railroads would also push their way across the western plains, and we turn now to the Northern Pacific and the Great Northern's race to be first to complete the first northern transcontinental route.

By 1880 railroads stretched across 93,267 miles in the United States, nearly double the total miles of track in 1870. The Santa Fe line now stretches through New Mexico and Arizona territories to the southern coast of California—creating a southwestern transcontinental route. Association of American Railroads

8

BUILDING A NORTHERN CROSSING
1864–1894

THE FIRST NORTHERN TRANSCONTINENTAL RAILROAD

Although violence and corruption tarnished the "golden age" of railroads, there was still a job to be done that only the railroads could do. Even after the Union Pacific and the Central Pacific met at Promontory in 1869, much of the West was still "unconnected," particularly the northwestern states.

Plans for the nation's first northern transcontinental railroad had begun with congressional authorization in 1864, two years after the mandate given to the Central Pacific and the Union Pacific. But setbacks delayed the start of construction until 1870—and the delay was indicative of the Northern Pacific's troubled history. Government legislation called for the line to begin at Lake Superior, in the east, and end at Puget Sound in the territory of Washington, in the west. Its route would roughly parallel the historic Lewis and Clark Trail and would run from Lake Superior across what are now the states of Minnesota, North Dakota, Montana, Idaho and Washington.

Because the territory was untamed and desolate, the government had given the Northern Pacific land grants amounting to 25,600 acres for every mile of track laid, or over 47 million acres in all. But the original authorization offered no government loans to help at the beginning, and the railroad was forbidden to mortgage either its land or its line to raise money. Raising money became a big problem, and construction couldn't actually begin until the authorization was revised to permit the railroad to mortgage land and to sell bonds.

Even so, the barren northwest expanses were less than promising—an unknown wilderness, populated by Indians, subject to extreme weather conditions. It was no easy task to convince potential investors that either the line or the land were worth anything—appearing, all in all, pretty unlikely to give anyone a healthy return on money put down.

The Northern Pacific decided to solve the problem through advertising. And while the railroad may have believed its own advertising in praise of the available lands, the promises sometimes bordered on the ludicrous. One circular even suggested that vast orange groves had been discovered in the desolate territory and that its climate could be compared to that of Paris or Venice.

Stretching the truth, though, may have seemed expedient to the NP directors, who suspected the rival Union Pacific of distributing a series of pamphlets that declared the Northwest was filled with barbarous Indians, plagued by an inhuman climate, teeming with dangerous wildlife and generally unfit for civilized human beings.

Somehow, the Northern Pacific managed to raise enough money—for a while—and construction began. Track crews began on both ends of the line at once and headed toward one another. The work went relatively smoothly until 1873, when financial panic played havoc with the nation's economy. Soon after the eastern end of the line had reached Bismarck, North Dakota, the NP got caught in the financial crunch, again ran out of money and was forced into bankruptcy. Not until several years later did new management and fresh money allow construction to resume.

Money wasn't the Northern Pacific's only problem, though. Much of the 47 million acres of land so generously allotted to the railroad was Indian land. And the northern tribes were no happier with the white man's invasion into their territory than their brothers on the Central Plains had been.

In fact, the NP's Indian problems were so severe that General George Armstrong Custer and the 7th Cavalry were brought in to protect the railroad's workers. Custer's orders were to subdue the tribes and move them safely out of the railroad's way and onto reservations. Unfortunately, the orders were easier to give than they were to execute. The railroad eventually won its battle through sheer persistence and the overwhelming influx of white settlers. But that was not until well after Custer and all his 266 men were killed at the famous Battle of the Little Bighorn in 1876.

As it continued to fight Indians and money troubles, the Northern Pacific proceeded slowly in its transcontinental trek. In the early 1880s, with only a few hundred miles left to close the gap, the NP again found itself in serious financial trouble. Temporary rescue this time came from an unlikely source, an ex-newspaper reporter and war correspondent named Henry Villard. Villard had become involved in railroading when friends in his native Germany asked him to look into some of their American railroad investments. He had acquired a small line of his own on the West Coast, the Oregon Railway and Navigation Company, with hopes of connecting up with the northern transcontinental when it reached the coast. Now with the NP approaching completion on a route farther north,

A Northern Pacific grading crew constructing the railroad's right-of-way in Dakota territory in 1879. Burlington Northern Railroad

At the railhead in Montana, 1887. In this year the St. Paul, Minneapolis & Manitoba (later part of the Great Northern) laid 698 miles of track between Minot, North Dakota and Helena, Montana in 201 days. To the right of the bridge the rails have been laid; to the left the right-of-way has been prepared. Teams in the background are hauling ties and other materials, and the horse at the extreme left is pulling the rail cars. Burlington Northern Railroad

Villard saw an opportunity much larger than he had originally planned. By borrowing money from wealthy friends, he purchased controlling shares in the entire NP line, rounded up thousands of Chinese workers to finish the last miles in the gap between eastbound and westbound tracks and found himself at the head of a railroad empire.

ANOTHER EMPIRE IN THE NORTH: THE GREAT NORTHERN

Villard's empire, though, had a competitor in the north. James Jerome Hill's Great Northern Railroad actually started to put itself together well before the Northern Pacific had even begun laying its tracks. An ambitious and energetic Canadian, Jim Hill emigrated to the United States in 1856. He found a job as a waterfront shipping clerk in St. Paul, Minnesota, educated himself and soon became an expert in trade and shipping. When the struggling little St. Paul and Pacific Railroad went into bankruptcy in 1878, Hill borrowed money and took it over. The SP&P's lineage stretched back to the 60-mile-long Minnesota and Pacific Railroad, founded in 1857

and taken over by the St. Paul and Pacific a few years later. The grandiose "and Pacific" in the names served only as a pathetic remainder of the original ambitious intentions of the two failed railroads. The Panic of 1873 had brought hard times, and a relentless plague of grasshoppers had blackened the skies and fouled the tracks.

The grasshopper plague blew over, however, and after repairing the ill-kept track and upgrading the line's equipment, Jim Hill soon had the SP&P back in business. It was a modest acquisition, although it took all the money he had on hand or could round up, but it was the beginning of his empire. Hill put his keen sense of trade to work by running a connecting line across the border and north to Winnipeg, Saskatchewan in Canada. Like others, he envisioned a line of rails that would stretch across the great American Northwest, tapping into its rich resources. "Most people who have really lived," he once said, "have had, in some shape, their great adventure. The railroad is mine."

Unlike the other transcontinental railroads, though, Hill's Great Northern would not be built with the help of government funds or land grants. Hill's

St. Paul, Minneapolis & Manitoba construction workers posed in front of one of the "skyscraper" dormitory cars used to house workers on the plains. When they reached the mountains, these cars had to be "sawed down" to tunnel size. Burlington Northern Railroad

philosophy was simple. He would put a transcontinental railroad together, but he would do it slowly, building where trade created a need for his railroad. By building spurs and buying short, connecting lines, he might take longer to complete his through route—but he would make his railroad pay for itself, as it was built.

On Jim Hill's railroad, no freight car would ever travel the rails empty. If there was a lumber mill that could be connected by his line, Hill would connect it, building dozens of branch lines across the state of Minnesota. From every corner of that state he collected and shipped wheat, helping to establish Minneapolis as the great milling center of the nation. In Montana he laid branches to the coal mines, using some of the coal on his own railroad and shipping the rest.

Connecting and branching, connecting again and branching again, Jim Hill's railroad often looked as if it were rambling in all directions at once. But under Hill's guidance it kept crawling slowly west. His involvement was keen and total. Said to know all his superintendents by name, he earned the respect of his men with his personal commitment. Many years later, Lee Howard, who had worked for Hill, recalled a typical incident to Stewart Holbrook. During a "sizable blizzard" in the late 1870s, Howard was working on a track gang in Dakota. He recalled:

Jim Hill came out in his special car to where a crew of us were trying to clear the line. He didn't stay in his car, either. He grabbed my shovel and started

tossing snow, telling me to go back to his car and I'd find a pot of coffee there. I did, and spent half an hour drinking coffee and resting. Mr. Hill spelled off first one man, then another. My, but he was tough!

Hill's railroad reached Great Falls, Montana in 1887. And sometime during 1890 Hill for the first time gave his railroad empire a name: the Great Northern.

Finally, in 1893, after driving a tunnel through the Cascade Mountains and crossing the Great Divide, the Great Northern made its final major connection—one that would at last finish what had started over 25 years before—to Seattle, Washington and the Pacific Coast.

Together the two great rivals, the Northern Pacific, finished in 1883, and the Great Northern, completed 10 years later, in 1893, fully opened up the great American Northwest. And, like the other great railroad lines crossing the midwestern and western states, they not only opened up the land but encouraged settlers to use it. The railroads needed people and goods to make them profitable, and Hill, like his rivals on the Northern Pacific, actively sought out homesteaders and ranchers, often as far away as England, Scotland, Ireland and Europe. He encouraged Swedish and Norwegian emigration and offered emigrants special deals and help in getting set up and started. The going was rough and many of the settlers quit, discouraged and beaten by the

---

Trains and Dates

ESTABLISHING THE NORTHERN ROUTES
1864–1894

1864   Congress authorizes the first northern transcontinental railroad, the Northern Pacific.

1870   Construction begins on the NP.

1873   The Panic of 1873 sends the NP into bankruptcy.

1876   While trying to protect the Northern Pacific Railroad, General George Custer and his entire unit are wiped out by Sioux and Cheyenne Indians at Little Bighorn, Montana.

1878   The St. Paul and Pacific Railroad goes into bankruptcy and James Hill buys the line.

1881   Henry Villard buys a controlling interest in the Northern Pacific.

1883   September. The midwestern and western legs of the NP are connected.

1887   Jim Hill's railroad, building westward, reaches Great Falls, Montana.

1890   Hill names his railroad the Great Northern.

1893   The Great Northern reaches Seattle, Washington on the Pacific Coast.

---

weather, Indians, the vagaries of economics or just plain bad luck. But many more stayed. And, in the end, not only the railroads thrived as a result, but the nation as well.

Not everyone agreed that Jim Hill was unequivocally the bearer of great good, of course. Once he had established a monopoly, he jacked up his prices, to the great anger of farmers along the route, who had no other way to transport their grain to the storage elevators and shipping docks. As one cynic put it, "After the grasshoppers, we had James Hill."

It was, for good or bad, the Golden Age of Railroading. A time of throwing tracks down, climbing over and through mountains, crossing rivers, prairies and deserts and building empires. A time of heroic visionaries and great and courageous engineering feats. It was also a time when the buffalo died, when the Indians were cheated and slaughtered and when crooked and greedy men made vast, illegal fortunes. It was the time of the settler and homesteader who depended on the railroad—and who were served by it, at times well and honestly, and at times badly, cruelly and corruptly.

It was a time of great booming industries made possible by thousands of thin lines of railroad tracks spreading in vast nets across the continent, bringing together the city and the country, the small town and the metropolis.

It was a time when it seemed that America and the railroad were, for good and for bad, one. And always would be.

But the times were changing.

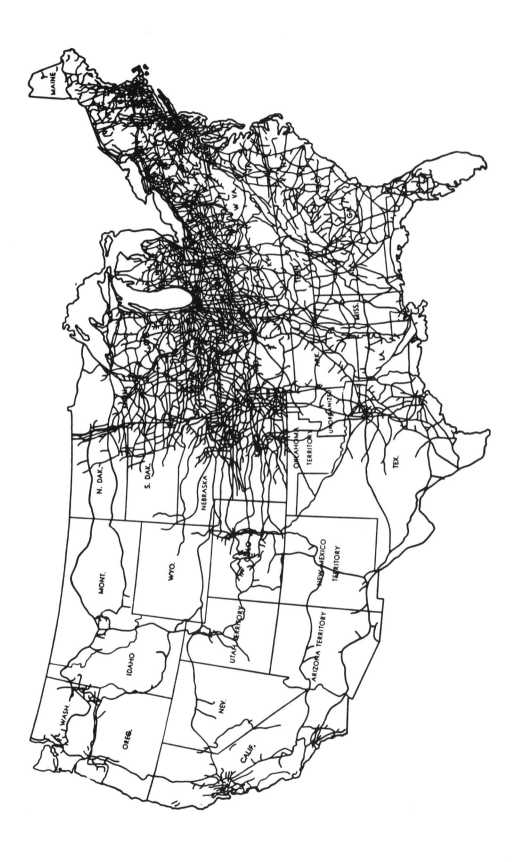

Map of the U.S. railway network in 1890 showing the two northern transcontinental routes then completed. More than 70,300 miles of new lines were opened between 1880 and 1890, bringing the total to 163,597 miles. Association of American Railroads

9

THE DECLINE BEGINS: RAILROADS 1914–1960

Between the turn of the century and the 1940s, the railroads reached the peak of their power and growth in the United States. By 1900 the total investment in railroads and railroad property was over $10 billion, a remarkable sum for those days, making the industry one of the richest and most powerful forces in American economic history. By 1916 over 254,000 miles of track were in operation. With its tracks, tunnels and bridges, the railroad had quite literally changed the face of the nation.

But forces that would lead to the railroad's slow and painful decline were already at work in those early years of the 20th century.

Not the least significant of these was the reputation that the railroads had created for themselves. Scandals and stories of corruption, bribery and graft continued to make the newspaper headlines. The transcontinentals had united the coasts and opened up the West and Midwest, but now many Americans believed that the government had given away too much of the vast new land to the railroad companies. The high-handed attitudes of the railroads toward the public didn't help matters, as prices fluctuated wildly and special favors were bought openly. More and more calls for government intervention and legislation rang throughout the land.

Also, at the same time that public opinion began to turn against railroads, it was turning toward a re-

markable new invention. In 1895 there were only four automobiles in the entire United States, and at the turn of the century, only 8,000. Five years later, in 1905, the number had jumped to 78,000. By 1915 there were 3,500,000 licensed motor vehicles. By 1925 the number had reached 20,000,000.

Spreading like wildfire, the automobile allowed Americans a degree of personal freedom and self-reliance that railroads could never offer. In 1903 an early Packard model became the first automobile to make a cross-country trip between San Francisco, California and New York City, and during the early 1900s such cross-country journeys, called "Ocean to Ocean," became a widely popular fad.

Even more ominous for the railroads, as early as 1907 a few enterprising men driving trucks were beginning to transport goods between nearby cities. Prior to World War I roads and highways were too poor for real long-distance hauling, but during the war the government began a spate of building and repairing. In 1915, the second year of the war, the number of trucks in the nation had jumped to 136,000, and by 1920 there were over a million cargo-carrying vehicles traveling roads and highways across the United States.

A second major transportation innovation, only slightly slower to develop, would also prove to be stiff competition for the railroads over the long haul. On December 17, 1903 Orville and Wilbur Wright proved

Pictured on the Canyon Diablo Bridge in Arizona in the early 20th century, the Santa Fe's all-first-class express, the California Limited, made fast time from Chicago to Los Angeles. Kansas State Historical Society

that machines could be made to fly. By 1919 the first daily airmail service between New York and Chicago had begun, and by 1924 service was available between New York and San Francisco. Air passenger service also began as early as the 1920s. Though more expensive, from the beginning airplanes could get anywhere faster than trains, and by the 1940s the competition for passenger service, especially, would become intense. Trying to offset the airline advantage, one Southern Pacific Railroad advertising brochure argued that it was unfair of airlines to compare one-way fares for rail and air. Much better, said SP, would be a comparison between two-way fares—since railroads offered a reduced round trip, while airlines didn't. And, the brochure continued, comparing sleeping car rates on a train with airline coach seats was like comparing a bed with a chair. As the ad complained: " . . . we wish they [the airlines] wouldn't spend so much time talking about railroads in their advertising. They seem to know so many things about railroad service that aren't so!"

The railroads, meanwhile, continued to refine their equipment and improve their operations, experimenting extensively with new types of locomotives and cars. Though motor vehicles and airplanes had begun to threaten the railroad's premier position, most of the first half of the century continued

to be a period of growth and improvement for travel and shipment by rail.

THE ELECTRIC BUZZ

Appropriately, the pioneering Baltimore and Ohio Railroad introduced the first American main-line electric locomotive. Put into service in 1895, the clean, quiet engine pulled cars through the city of Baltimore and its Howard Street Tunnel. Like many other eastern lines, the B&O had begun to face serious opposition to running its ever-bigger locomotives through city centers. Belching immense quantities of smoke and steam, the big engines were fine for conquering the miles between the cities but proved a nuisance and a danger within city limits. And tunnels compounded the problem. Not only were crews and passengers plagued by the thick smoke trapped inside the tunnels, but visibility was often so bad that the train crews couldn't see the track directly in front of the locomotive.

The B&O's electric locomotive solved that problem, drawing its power from an overhead wire rather than by burning coal, and it was also capable of hauling extremely heavy loads, sometimes including the steam engine that had pulled its passengers and cargo cars between cities.

Trains and Dates

1914–1960

1917 December 28. Wartime emergency called by federal government, which takes control of railroads.

1920 March 1. The Transportation Act of 1920 returns control of the railroads to railroad owners. The act also encourages mergers formerly opposed by the federal government.

1925 The first diesel-electric locomotive (a switcher) is put in service.

1927 The first centralized traffic control (CTC) is established (on 40-mile route near Berwick, Ohio). By 1980 CTC is installed on 53,000 miles of track, providing electric control of train movement, through switches and signals, from a centralized location.

1928 West of Denver, the Moffat Tunnel, at 6.2 miles the longest in the United States at the time, opens to train traffic.

1929 January 12. The Great Northern's 7.73-mile Cascade Tunnel opens in Washington State. It is the longest in the Western Hemisphere.

The first air-conditioned Pullman is introduced, running between Los Angeles and Chicago.

1931 The Baltimore & Ohio introduces the first air-conditioned train on its run between Washington and New York.

1934 May 26. First streamlined diesel-electric train makes nonstop run from Denver to Chicago.

November 11. First regular streamlined passenger service begins.

The American Railroad Association is formed.

1937 The first two-way telephone communication on a train takes place between Albion, Pennsylvania and Pittsburgh.

Federal Railroad Retirement Act went into effect, creating mandatory retirement programs and other benefits for railroad workers.

1941 First diesel-electric road freight locomotives are placed in regular service.

1944 Railroad passenger traffic reaches an all-time high of 95.6 billion passenger miles, after which the competition of air traffic and automobiles causes a decline.

1945 The Federal Communications Commission (FCC) allocates radio channels for exclusive railroad use.

The first modern domed observation car is introduced, running between Chicago and Minneapolis.

September 2. World War II use of railroads draws to a close with V-J Day. The railroads have operated nearly 114,000 troop trains during the three years nine months of war, and were heavily used by the military for moving freight within the United States.

1949 On a 106-mile route in Kansas, the first long-distance microwave communications system is installed by a railroad.

1952 The first gas-turbine-electric locomotive built and operated in the United States goes into regular service.

By now American railroads own more diesel-electric locomotives than steam locomotives.

1955 An electronic computer is installed for the first time in the railroad industry.

The electric locomotive wasn't new; it was already in use on some specialized short lines in England and Europe, but the Baltimore and Ohio was the first American railroad to use one as a part of its main-line service.

The problems of smoke-filled tunnels also brought the electric locomotive to New York City in 1902. As an incoming train entered the two-and-a-half-mile-long Park Avenue Tunnel, smoke obscured the red signal that warned of a stationary train on the tracks ahead. The two-train collision killed 15 people. There had been previous problems in the tunnel, and after this accident the city drew up a ban on steam locomotives running within the city limits, which went into effect in 1908. By the time the Pennsylvania Railroad had completed its new Pennsylvania Station in New York City in 1909, its trains were running on electrified track, using a direct-current (dc) third rail, through tunnels under the Hudson and East rivers. The third rail was later replaced by an alternating-current (ac) overhead wire. And when the Grand Central Terminal opened in New York in 1913, the New York Central railway extended its electric track along the Hudson River to Harmon, 33 miles away.

Other lines were also experimenting with electricity. In 1917 the last transcontinental to be built—the Chicago, Milwaukee, St. Paul and Pacific Railroad—electrified 483 miles of its track over the Rocky Mountains between Harlowton and Avery, Montana. It added another 230 miles of electrification from Othello to Tacoma, Washington in 1919. The experiments were successful and the extra power, efficiency and speed of the electrics were impressive. But not so impressive was the cost of building and running electrified track over such long distances. With operating costs spiraling higher and the new gadget called the automobile threatening their revenues, most of the railroads decided to use electricity only when needed and then only on much shorter stretches of track.

Then too, in those early years of the 20th century, there was a much bigger problem looming on the horizon.

WORLD WAR I AND THE NATIONALIZATION OF THE RAILROADS

Although war broke out in Europe in 1914, the United States was initially hesitant to get involved. When the United States finally entered the conflict in 1917, the railroads were thrown into chaos and confusion. In April 1917 industry executives hastily organized the Railway War Board in an attempt to coordinate the massive traffic of supplies that would have to be shipped back and forth across the nation as part of the war effort. The voluntary move, though, was an abysmal failure.

More used to competing than cooperating and still stuck with old habits of favoritism toward specific customers, the railroads simply couldn't handle the sudden changes in priority the government demanded. Special priority "tags" issued by the government to be affixed to cargoes of much-needed war supplies were often given to nonpriority shippers who were valued old-time customers. Railroad cars were packed and then often sidetracked to sit waiting beside the main lines while "favored" cargoes took their place.

The situation was chaotic and bottlenecked. At one point it was estimated that over 180,000 fully loaded railroad cars were sitting idly on sidings across the United States while the railroads were reporting that they were 158,000 cars short of the number needed to fulfill their war-related obligations.

To many citizens, incensed by press reports of the railroad chaos, it looked as if it was just the "same old railroads, up to the same old tricks."

In December 1917 authorized by the Federal Possession and Control Act of 1916, which allowed the government to control and operate railroad lines in wartime, the United States government stepped in, took over and set up the U.S. Railroad Administration (USRA). Essentially, the government forcibly "leased" all the major railroad facilities (except for interurban, city transit or industrial railroads) and brought them under strict and centralized control for the duration of the war.

The move quickly made the railroads more efficient. Under government control and centralization, much peacetime "fat" was trimmed away as locomotives and cars were standardized, purchasing centralized and operations pooled and coordinated.

The railroads ran efficiently, but, as calculated after the war, they also ran at a financial loss. Higher wages given to railroad employees, new equipment purchased under rising prices and a freeze on increased freight rates cost the rail industry nearly $2 million a day during the 26 months that it was under government management.

MORE CHANGES IN STORE FOR THE RAILROAD AND THE NATION

The Transportation Act of 1920 returned the railroads to private ownership and management.

Technology Close-Up

THE DIESEL LOCOMOTIVE—AND HOW IT WORKS

When the Burlington's streamlined diesel Zephyr streaked across the Midwest in 1934, it symbolized the coming of a new age, a time when trains shaped like sleek bullets would replace the chugging, smoke- and cinder-spewing steam engine. Soon it was joined by others with such names as Comet, Meadowlark, Meteor, Super Chief and Flying Yankee. Not everyone welcomed the diesel—for many the steam engine had more romance and charm—but the diesel had strong advantages. Less noisy and cleaner, the diesel locomotive offered much higher fuel efficiency. The diesel was faster and more powerful, nearly unaffected by cold weather and could travel as much as 6,000 miles with minimal maintenance. And in an age of increasing air travel, the clean lines of the diesel's look were more contemporary (some steam engines were even disguised to look like diesels).

The most common type of diesel locomotive is the diesel-electric, in which the diesel engine powers a dynamo, which in turn powers electric motors to turn the wheels. The locomotive runs on diesel fuel, which is sprayed into a cylinder of compressed air. There it ignites with the heat of compression. Expanding gases from the explosion drive a piston in the cylinder, which in turn drives the electric dynamo. Power from the dynamo moves the locomotive.

From the cab in the controlling locomotive, a single engineer can run several diesel locomotives doubleheaded, or teamed together, to pull a train. And one drop of diesel fuel can pull a 100-ton freight car 8 inches. As railroad historian Freeman Hubbard put it, "there is little doubt that the diesel saved American railroads from ruin after World War II." While the diesel locomotive could not alone succeed in saving the railroads, it greatly increased their ability to provide 20th-century trains with the power they needed.

Much was changing, though, for both the railroads and the nation as a whole. Increasing public demand for tighter government regulation of the railroads after the war was over had stiffened already existing controls at the same time the lines were restored to private management. Built into the Transportation Act was authorization for the Interstate Commerce Commission to require railroads to establish and maintain rates that would yield a "fair return"—not necessarily the vast profits of previous years. The act also empowered the ICC to set rates and to establish the Railway Labor Board.

The railroad unions had become stronger and larger and were putting pressure on the lines from within, demanding better wages, shorter hours and better working conditions.

Operating costs meanwhile had continued to rise. And many small lines, caught in the squeeze, collapsed or were absorbed by their larger and more successful competitors. The larger lines also were struggling. The success of the automobile had stoked up a demand for more and better roads, and now they began to be built. The new ribbons of asphalt cut not only into railroad revenues but into railroad territory as well.

Now a new group of moguls were slowly coming into the picture, the automobile manufacturers. Private investments in railroads began to decline as investors turned toward the promising new automobile industry.

Still, it wasn't time to count the railroads out yet.

As America moved painfully into the depression years of the 1930s and early '40s, the railroads fought, as did most of the rest of the nation, to stay alive in the economic upheaval.

New equipment and more economical techniques were developed, including steel box cars to replace wooden ones, continuously welded rails for smoother and more efficient running, improved refrigerator cars for carrying perishable goods, more comfortable passenger cars, two-way radio communications between trains and dispatch offices, and automated freight yards.

Much of the railroad's success during this period, though, was due to the diesel engine.

DAYS OF THE STREAMLINER

Although companies in England, Europe and America had been experimenting with diesel technology for a number of years, the first "commercially successful" diesel (see box) was put on the tracks regularly in 1925. Instead of using the expansion of steam, formed by heating water with burning wood or coal, diesel locomotives use the force of diesel fuel ignited under compression. The resulting power usually drives an electric dynamo to move the train. The new diesel was powerful and efficient, used, like the externally powered electric locomotives that came before it, almost exclusively for short hauls. But, also like the electric, it was expensive to run. Still, over the next four years, 26 of these diesel-electrics went into regular operation on such eastern lines as the ever-pioneering Baltimore and Ohio, the Central of New Jersey and the Reading.

The historic breakthrough for diesel-powered locomotives came 10 years later, in 1934. On May 26 of that year a sleek, streamlined, stainless-steel diesel-electric took to the tracks between Denver, Colorado and Chicago, Illinois. Making the trip in just over 13 hours, The Pioneer Zephyr broke the world's record for speed between those two cities. And as it pulled into its destination, The Century of Progress Exhibition in Chicago, a new era in American railroading was born. The Zephyr looked completely unlike any engine that had come before it, and with its incredible speed and futuristic design the new streamliner took the nation by storm. Besides offering speed, this passenger's delight also featured comfortably air-conditioned cars, reclining seats, a grill-buffet and an observation lounge. It was a model, quite literally. No others would ever be built exactly like it, but from then on few engines would be built completely differently. The diesel train had come to stay.

The development of double-duty, freight-and-passenger diesel-electrics in the late 1930s spelled the end of the steam era on American railroads. Although a few independent short lines continued to operate by steam, the days of the colorful smoke engines were over. As Bill Within put it in an article for *Trains* magazine, "In its fight for survival during the 1940s, the steam locomotive lost by default." By the outbreak of World War II, the diesel locomotive had become dominant on American railways.

The Burlington's Pioneer Zephyr, America's first diesel-powered streamline train, began operation April 9, 1934. Association of American Railroads

WORLD WAR II: THE LAST HURRAH OF AMERICAN RAILROADS

World War I, which had been called "the war to end all wars," unfortunately hadn't. By the early 1940s, as the United States found itself again being drawn into war, the railroads had decided to prepare. Beginning in 1940, the railroads began building tens of thousands of locomotives and even more rolling stock in anticipation of increased demands on their resources. Even before the United States entered the war, the railroads carried tons of munitions, food and clothing to ports for shipment to war-torn areas of Europe. By the time the United States declared war on December 8, 1941, the railroads were ready—and this time, by cooperating closely with the military, they were able to avoid government control. Although the government intervened during the war years during a few strikes and strike threats, the railroads were left pretty much in the hands of private management.

From one point of view, business boomed. During the four years of war, rail cargo jumped by over 50%, with railroads handling 90% of all freight traffic. And the military relied on the rails for 98% of all travel required for military personnel within the country— to training camps, to military posts, to points of embarkation. This time the railroads functioned with relative speed and efficiency, thanks in part to technological advances since World War I and in part to the railroads' determination to avoid another government seizure. Although the American railroads lost some 350,000 workers who were called up or enlisted for military service during the war, like many other industries, they replaced many of them—at least until the men returned—by hiring women.

In a sense business was so good that the railroads launched an active campaign to discourage passenger travel—especially during the holidays and other peak travel times when they needed to reserve their capacity for military troops. With servicemen traveling constantly, on pass or in troop movements, demand for transportation had greatly increased. Despite the campaign, passenger traffic picked up dramatically as gasoline and tire shortages forced many Americans to travel by rail rather than automobile. Many lines, large and small, which had been struggling to remain solvent soon found themselves turning profits again.

By 1950 railroads had formed a dense transportation network connecting virtually every populated area throughout the nation. The challenge now became not construction but developing new, more efficient ways to use the network already formed. Association of American Railroads

Passenger travel by rail during the war did have its drawbacks, though. The cars were jammed with soldiers and sailors. Passengers faced crowded stations, always-busy public telephones, long ticket lines and late trains. Observation cars and sleeping cars, commandeered for troop movement, became a luxury of the past. Dining cars, when included on a train, usually served poorly prepared meals. But along with increased taxes, scarce supplies and rationing, most people saw these hardships as just another aspect of the burden of war—caused, as the railroad advertising copywriters declared, by the aggressions of the German leader Adolf Hitler and Japan's Emperor Hirohito.

With the end of the war, though, came another story. The financial boom of the war years—with revenues nearly double what they had been in 1918—turned out to be the railroads' last hurrah. They had carried more people and freight than ever before. But by the end of the late 1940s, with the transportation boom created by the war now over, most railroads were in financial trouble again. Steel shortages and production limitations during the war had kept the railroads from building and improving diesel locomotives and had kept the steam locomotive manufacturers from researching ways to combat the encroachment of the diesel engine. As a result, at the war's end, the railroads were even less well equipped to compete in the changing transportation climate in which truck, auto and airplane created new challenges. Ironically too, because the military made use of the railroads at reduced rates up until October 1946, the railroads made less money per traveled mile than they otherwise would have. Now, as travelers and shippers turned to other forms of transportation, for many of the nation's lines, the great age of American railroading had come to an end.

10

THE AGE OF MERGERS: CONRAIL AND AMTRAK 1960 TO THE 1990s

In March 1950 General Motors, an automobile manufacturer, announced earnings for 1949 of $656,434,232, the largest profit made in one year by an American corporation up to that time. Over roads and highways across the nation, millions of automobiles, trucks and buses now scurried daily like busy, bustling ants. Efficient and inexpensive cross-country bus service had begun to cut into the railroads' passenger traffic, and, although railroads were slow to recognize the change, America had unquestionably found another way of getting there.

By now the railroads also met with fierce competition from the airline industry. The airplane, like the automobile, had grown up almost overnight to become an integral part of the American way of life. In 1930, when the first commercial transcontinental passenger flight took to the air between Los Angeles and New York City, the railroads had paid little notice. The fledgling airline industry cut into railroad passenger traffic by less than 1% that year. But by the late 1940s the picture had drastically changed. After struggling through the depression and their own growing pains, the airlines had become the favored means of long-distance transportation for many travelers. By 1948 over 13 million passengers a year were making the choice to get there faster—by air.

In much the same way that the railroads had drained the life from the canals, so motor vehicles and airplanes were draining the life from the railroads.

Despite heavy competition from the trucking industry, however, railroads still had the biggest share of American freight traffic. And now they focused most of their attention on freight. With a passenger-be-damned attitude that had actually started soon after the railroads began to discover the great profit to be had in freight, the lines continued to let their passenger services deteriorate while they struggled against one another for freight contracts.

Expenses, though, were becoming higher almost daily, and government regulations were severely limiting the railroads' competitive edge. By the 1960s railroads began to find themselves in serious trouble.

A WAVE OF CONSOLIDATIONS

The once-great and colorful map of American railroads had begun to change its form, as the mighty rails that had conquered the continent now struggled desperately to stay alive. In a last-ditch effort, many of the old lines in the eastern United States tried to cut expenses by consolidating, joining together to save themselves from financial ruin. In 1960 the famous

Amtrak's Empire State Express speeding passengers along the Hudson River between New York City and Niagara Falls. Amtrak

Erie railroad joined with the Delaware, Lackawanna & Western to form a new line, the Erie Lackawanna Railroad Company. The merger was a sign of the future, with continuing consolidations throughout the 1960s, '70s and '80s. Many lines that couldn't consolidate, or refused to, went into bankruptcy. In 1967 the Central Railroad of New Jersey fell into the hands of the bankruptcy court. Hoping to avoid the same fate, the once-powerful New York Central Railroad and its equally powerful rival, the Pennsylvania Railroad, joined together to form the Penn Central Transportation Company in 1968. The move came too late, though, and the Penn Central filed for bankruptcy in 1970.

The Chesapeake and Ohio bought out the historic Baltimore and Ohio, becoming the Chessie System. The Norfolk and Western took over the Virginian, the colorful Wabash and the Nickel Plate. Some consolidations were successful, while others only offered a temporary reprieve. The Erie Lackawanna merger stalled fate by only a few years, and by 1972 that line too fell into the hands of the courts.

While the heavily competitive eastern lines were hardest hit by failure, the wave of desperate consolidations and mergers also spilled westward. In 1970 two more great railroads and one-time rivals, the

historic Great Northern and Northern Pacific railways, merged with the Chicago Burlington and Quincy and the Spokane, Portland and Seattle railroads to create the Burlington Northern. In the next 10 years the Burlington would absorb a half-dozen other lines to become one of the largest single lines in the United States, second only to the CSX Corporation, which itself was formed in 1980 by merging the Chessie System with nearly a dozen other struggling eastern and midwestern lines. In 1982 the Union Pacific, Missouri Pacific and Western Pacific merged to form the Union Pacific Corporation, and the Union Pacific bought the Missouri-Kansas-Texas in 1988. Also in 1988, Rio Grande Industries bought the Southern Pacific.

AMTRAK AND CONRAIL

In the early days, perhaps, the government had kept its hands off too long and had let the railroads go too far. But then, in trying to prevent repetitions of the scandals and corruption of the past, too much federal regulation had effectively placed a stranglehold on the industry. Now, after the collapse of the gigantic Penn Central System in 1970, the United States government stepped in once more. The result was the

These truck trailers "piggybacking" aboard Santa Fe flatcars illustrate just one form of intermodal transportation methods that railroads are using to provide better service in today's competitive transportation market. Santa Fe Railway

formation of Amtrak (also known as the National Railroad Passenger Corporation or NRPC) and Conrail (the Consolidated Rail Corporation) in the early 1970s.

Created by the Rail Passenger Service Act in 1970, Amtrak is a semipublic corporation that took over the operation of most of the nation's passenger service cross-country and between cities. Provisions of the act allowed railroads to discontinue passenger service, turning over their passenger equipment to Amtrak. The tracks used by Amtrak, though, remained privately owned by the various railroad lines.

Operated by a board of directors, some representing stockholders and some appointed by the government, Amtrak is financed by a combination of its own revenues and government aid. By 1970, most railroads were eager to drop their passenger business in order to focus on the more profitable freight traffic. Louis Menk, who was chairman of the board at Burlington Northern and an Amtrak board member in the early 1970s, spoke for many in railroad upper management when he said of the passenger train, "It's time to let it die an honorable death."

Amtrak's early days were marred by inefficiencies. One would-be passenger sent a letter to the

editor of the *New York Times* in 1974 in which she recounted verbatim a telephone conversation she had with an Amtrak ticket agent. The 5:00 train from New York to Philadelphia, he told her, arrived at 5:30. Well, actually, he admitted when pressed, the arrival time was 6:30. Did it stop in North Philadelphia? Oh, yes. At 6:30. Again, when questioned, he clarified that the North Philadelphia stop was 10 minutes later. Finally he admitted that the North Philadelphia stop was not made by the Amtrak train at all, but by a Penn Central train that also departed from New York at 5:00. For further information, he added, "You have to call Penn Central." It's not clear whether the caller ever made the trip.

Conrail, established by the Rail Revitalization and Regulatory Reform Act of 1975, was formed as a privately managed corporation set up to take over the Penn Central and a large group of other bankrupt eastern railroads. Operating in the Northeastern Corridor (between Washington, D.C. and Boston), its primary function is to carry freight through the heavily industrialized states. Unlike Amtrak, Conrail (after an original federal subsidy of $2 billion) was organized to run without continuing government subsidies. In April 1987 Conrail was returned to the

---

Technology Close-Up

THE IRON HORSE AND THE SILICON CHIP: TRAINS AND COMPUTERS

Given the complexity of railroad operations, trains and computers make a natural team. And, in fact, as far back as 1809, Herman Hollerith set up a rudimentary punch-card system to tabulate data for use by a railroad. Only in recent years, however, have railroads really begun to tap the computer's tremendous potential.

A new generation of locomotives rides the rails today, sporting onboard computers that keep watch over speed, acceleration and braking. These "smart" locomotives also watch out for and diagnose mechanical problems when they arise.

By 1964 a freight yard in East St. Louis, Illinois had set a computer to work. There it sorted 2,500 freight cars daily, as they moved through the busy yard. Today most major freight yards are managed by computer. As a train rolls into the yard, information about its makeup (types of cars), known as its *consist*, is sent to the yard computer. Computers control the switches in the yard to sort the cars for the consist of outbound trains as they're being made up. The consist of outbound trains is then passed on to the railroad's main computer, which updates car movements and sends the information on to the next yard.

Railroads also use computers to keep data about maintenance for both track and equipment as well as for scheduling maintenance. Rail car tracing and billing are done by computer. And electronic data exchange—an electronic system for sending bills of lading, freight bills, way bills, purchase orders, invoices and other information—has changed the way the railroad industry does business. Eliminating volumes of paper, data travels swiftly from computer to computer across the country.

In the 1990s railroads look forward to an improvement over their current Central Train Control (CTC), which monitors trains' locations and movements by computer and controls signals to them. The new Advanced Train Control Systems (ATCS) will increase efficiency and safety by combining electronics, computers and telecommunications to control the flow of traffic across an entire railroad system. In combination with onboard computers, the ATCS will be able to keep locomotives moving safely. Transponders along the track will also pick up information as the train passes over them and send it on to the central computer, which will sort out any conflicts and give orders for routing.

From computer modeling and research, to operations control and data management, the railroad has made friends with the computer for keeps.

---

private sector in what was known as "the largest initial public stock offering of a U.S. industrial company in history." As a result, the federal government was relieved of 85% of its financial responsibilities for the railroad. Running strictly on its own profit, though, has proved difficult and Conrail, despite some success, has continued to find the going rough.

THE STAGGERS ACT OF 1980

Meanwhile, in 1980, hoping to keep the struggling railroads alive, Congress passed the Staggers Rail Act. This legislation, long awaited by railroad interests, loosened strict government controls and economic regulation. The idea was to provide railroads with the opportunity to find a competitive place once again in the varied American transportation network. The goal was to restore them to financial self-sufficiency.

The Staggers Act made it possible for railroads to compete with less-regulated trucks and barges and to be more flexible in a varied and changing transportation market. And railroads were now permitted to negotiate confidential contracts with their customers, a standard practice in most industries but previously not permitted to railroads.

As a result, in the afterglow of the Staggers Act, railroads spent tens of billions of dollars on rebuilding and revitalizing their systems and operations. Trains

Trains and Dates

RAILROADS APPROACH THE 21ST CENTURY
1960 TO THE 1990S

1962   The *Telstar* satellite transmits railroad information from St. Louis, Missouri to Dallas, Texas.

1965   Federal legislation authorizes a joint railroad-government program for high-speed transportation in the Northeast Corridor (Washington to Boston).

1966   The Interstate Commerce Commission gives the go-ahead for the merger of the New York Central and the Pennsylvania railroads, biggest merger in American history.

1969   First run of the high-speed Metroliner rail service between Washington, D.C. and New York.

          Turbo Train service is inaugurated between New York and Boston.

1970   Birth of Amtrak, the National Railroad Passenger Corporation. After 1971 most intercity passenger service in the United States is run by Amtrak.

1972   Passenger traffic on the railroads has dropped to 8.6 billion passenger miles, from 95.6 billion in 1944.

1976   Conrail (Consolidated Rail Corporation) begins operations. Mandated by Congress, the new railroad is the result of a consolidation of six bankrupt railroads.

1979   A fuel crisis causes an increase in rail passenger traffic to a 10-year high of 11.3 billion passenger miles.

1980   The Staggers Act of 1980 goes into effect, greatly reducing regulation of railroads.

          Nineteen railroads are now using long-distance microwave communications systems over 41,500 miles.

          Only 12 steam locomotives remain, with 28,483 diesel-electric locomotives in service.

          Freight traffic on Class I railroads reaches 918 billion revenue ton miles.

1983   Piggybacking boosts railroad revenues, with more than 4 million loaded containers and trailers moved via piggyback in one year.

1987   Conrail is returned to private sector, with the federal government retaining only 15% of its share in the railroad.

1988   Due to Staggers Act provisions that facilitate sales of light-density lines, 205 new railroads are operating by the end of the year.

1989   Nearly 6 million piggyback trailers and containers are loaded in one year, a record for the eighth successive year.

1990   Railroads begin to enjoy a boom in passenger-rail business, with a marked increase in travel by rail for pleasure.

          Ohio considers a rapid-rail passenger system between Cincinnati, Columbus and Cleveland, with plans for trains traveling between 160 mph and 200 mph.

that had been creeping along at 10 mph on old, damaged track now sped at 70 mph down rehabilitated rails. Gone were the days when car shortages delayed shipments, and deliveries began to arrive on time once again.

Whether, as some believe, all this is too little too late remains to be seen.

NEW STRATEGIES FOR PROFITABLE RAILROADING

By the 1990s America's economy has shifted its focus from heavy industry, which the railroad once served so effectively, to service and information industries. As a result, to survive, railroads must constantly innovate and respond to the needs of industry in order to hang on to their share of what industrial freight business still remains.

As William Reichard, of Bethlehem Steel Corporation, says, "What killed railroads in the past was inconsistent service. It used to be that one shipment would be delivered in three days, another in five days and a third would get lost and take 10 days for delivery." As of 1990, he says, "They've cleaned up those problems."

Technology has transformed the world of the railroad, from the introduction of satellite communications in 1962 to the constant refinement of equipment and management. Extensive research and computer systems development (see box) have helped railroads improve systems and find ways to improve train control and operation, eliminate time-consuming steps, reduce fuel consumption and increase service. For example, railroads have paid as much as $3 billion annually in fuel and other costs to move empty freight cars a total of some 10 million miles annually. But now a computer model developed by the Federal Railway Administration and Princeton University plots the most efficient routes, cutting the "empty" miles dramatically and saving some $9 million a year.

"Piggybacking," or intermodal shipping, which railroads have used for more than 25 years, has become the backbone of railroad freight shipment in recent years, with nearly 6 million containers riding piggyback in 1989. Containers designed to travel on ship, plane, truck trailer or train can be filled with wine, grain, or any other cargo and can be shipped part of the way by any or all of these transportation modes (hence the term "intermodal"). When traveling by train the containers are loaded "piggyback" on a flat car or on a special frame on wheels, then unloaded at the destination, often onto another truck, plane or ship. The piggyback system eliminates the need to unload and reload the contents of the container, which remain packed from origin to destination—saving time and preventing breakage and loss.

LOOKING TOWARD THE FUTURE

By 1990 the Staggers Act and the use of innovative improvements appeared to be turning the tide for the railroads.

By the end of the 1980s, railroads moved 60% of the country's new automobiles, nearly 60% of the coal, about 45% of the steel and about 26% of the grain. They are the most frequently used mode of transportation for shipping paper products, lumber and wood products and chemicals. In 1988 railroads had one of the most profitable years in rail history, though their rate of return on investment was still below the average for all U.S. industries. Meanwhile, since the Staggers Act, rates have risen less than they did in the three years before its passage, not even rising as fast as inflation. As one spokesperson for the American Railroad Association remarked, "We're not out of the woods yet, but at least we're not going under like we were."

The early 1990s also saw a renewed passenger boom in recreational railroad travel. As reported by *Time* magazine, about 4.8 million passengers toured the country on specialty trains, often steam-powered and decorated to recall the days of gold-rush travel in the Colorado mountains or the sumtuous passenger cars of the 1930s and '40s in Texas. What the railroads have going for them these days, oddly, is time—for short hauls, the speed and comfort of the rails versus the hassle and torment of clogged freeways; for long distances, a leisurely pace, disconnected from the hurly-burly of 1990s city life. Life seems to slow to a mesmerizing sway once you climb aboard a train, and, as one Texas limited passenger told *Time*, "People get on board thinking that two hours will be too long. But by the time they get off, they're old friends." Says dining-car waiter Jimmie Dean, "The ride is a little like buying a fire truck for a child: instant love."

Meanwhile, cities are recognizing the environmental advantages and traffic relief that rapid rail transit can bring. In the 1930s a campaign to "motorize downtown Los Angeles" succeeded in removing the

1,164 miles of Pacific Electric System track that had connected the world's largest interurban electric railway system. Today Los Angeles is desperately trying to reverse the trend, and nearly every urban area in the United States has built or is considering a rapid transit system to relieve the volume of commuter traffic on its highways. In Ohio, high-speed passenger trains may transform travel between Cincinnati, Columbus and Cleveland, if a pending plan goes through for express trains that travel at a speed of 160 mph to 200 mph.

Some railway experts also expect to see high-speed passenger trains that ride on magnetic cushions in this country within the next 10 or 20 years. Called magnetic levitation (maglev) trains, they would travel as fast as 300 mph, suspended above powerful magnetic fields. Robert J. Casey, executive director of the High Speed Rail Association, says he believes "there will be many thousands of miles of maglev and other high-speed trains in the next 20 years in North America."

Almost totally automated, this yard tower on the Norfolk Southern line in Linwood, North Carolina is designed to handle traffic to and from the Caroliinas and Virginia with speed and accuracy (though, for safety, a human operator can override the automated equipment). The Norfolk Southern has seven modern, computerized classification yards like this one, which can track thousands of care a week coming into the yard, assign them to new trains and get them out again and on their way. Association of American Railroads.

EPILOGUE

For more than a century railroads dominated transportation in the United States. And to this day the country maintains a passionate love affair—at times a love-hate relationship—with the railroads. During their greatest period of growth, they symbolized national economic strength and expansion. They created possibilities—ways to get crops to market, people to destinations, raw materials to factories and manufactured goods wherever they could be used. Wherever railroads reached, they encouraged farming, supported industry and connected distant lives. The health of the nation and the health of the railroad seemed one. Most of all, for the wandering American spirit, they meant mobility—as commentator Lowell Thomas once said, "America in motion." The belching smokestack, the haunting whistle, the clickety-clack and the endless rails of steel spoke of power and destiny, of romance and adventure, of future and fortune.

The power and the hiss of the steam engine captured the imagination, overcame vast distances and connected shore to shore. As the effervescent British actress Fanny Kemble wrote in 1830, it was a "magical machine with its wonderful flying white breath and rhythmical unvarying pace." Legends, mystique and nostalgia came to surround the railroads—exalted in such songs as "The Ballad of Casey Jones," "Paddy Works on the Erie," "Chattanooga Choo-Choo" and "The City of New Orleans." "You can hear the whistle blow," as the folk song says, "a hundred miles."

The dark underbelly of the railroad's success and romance—the corruption and ugliness of corporate greed—nearly led to its downfall. Outraged public reaction placed crippling checks on an industry that could and should have served the economy well into the 21st century. Today, struggling to overcome the past, America's railroads travel a tough route, often using, as historian Oliver Jensen puts it, "Buck Rogers equipment on Casey Jones tracks."

But despite the railroad's checkered legacy, America continues its love affair with the train. The sway of the coach, the hum of the rails, the ribbons of track plunge deep into the heart and soul of the countryside. Into a rural America of rippling wheat, rocky streams and steep mountainsides. Into vast deserts of arroyos and sagebrush. Through suburbs and cities, past towns and villages, past wrecking yards and old shacks, fast-food restaurants and schoolyards, shopping centers and asphalt seas. Commuter trains pierce the sultry rush-hour traffic, freight trains speed from supplier to market, passenger trains wind across the land, and still today the railroad remains a powerful symbol of human ability to conquer space and time. Spiritually, as the 19th-century novelist Nathaniel Hawthorne once put it, "They give us wings."

GLOSSARY

air brake A method of stopping or slowing that operates using compressed air.

block A length or section of track the use of which is controlled by signals and/or switches.

boiler The part of a steam locomotive in which steam is produced.

boxcar A rectangular freight car that is fully enclosed, like a box.

caboose Usually the last car on a train, used for the conductor's office and living quarters. Now that most trains use computerized controls, fewer trains include a caboose.

Class I Railroad A classification of railroads determined by the Interstate Commerce Commission, based on a railroad's annual revenues. In 1983 Class I Railroads were those with annual revenues of about $82 million.

colliery A coal mine and its buildings.

consist The makeup of a train—including the number and types of cars.

coupler A device for connecting two railroad cars.

doubleheaded Describes two locomotives teamed together (for extra power) at the head of a train.

firebox The part of a steam locomotive boiler where the fuel burns.

flatcar A freight car having no side rails or walls, just a flat platform.

gauge On a railroad track, the distance between the running edges of the rail (the edges the train travels on). Standard gauge in the United States is 4 feet 8½ inches.

intermodal transportation Transportation that combines rail transport with other means, such as air, truck or ship.

land grant A grant of land made by the government.

main line The trunk of a railroad network, used by its fastest, long-haul trains.

piggybacking The practice of carrying a container or truck trailer on a railroad car, such as a flatcar.

rolling stock All wheeled vehicles used by a railroad, including locomotives and cars.

tender The car carrying fuel and water that attaches to a locomotive.

sleeping car A passenger car that provides beds for sleeping.

tie Horizontal pieces placed between the rails to keep them at the proper gauge distance and to help distribute weight of the trains. They can be made of wood, steel, concrete or stone.

turbine A kind of rotary engine in which blades attached to a central shaft are turned by hot, expanding gases.

BIBLIOGRAPHY

Berkman, Pamela, ed. *The History of the Atchison, Topeka & Santa Fe.* Greenwich, Conn.: Bonanza, 1988.

Billings, Henry. *Bridges.* New York: Viking, 1956.

Botkin, B. A., and Alvin F. Harlow, eds. *A Treasury of Railroad Folklore.* New York: Bonanza Books, 1989.

Bowman, Hank Wieand. *Pioneer Railroads.* New York: Arco, 1954.

Bruchey, Stuart. *The Wealth of the Nation: An Economic History of the United States.* New York: Harper & Row, 1988.

Bryant, Keith L., Jr. *History of the Atchison, Topeka and Santa Fe Railroad.* New York: Macmillan, 1974.

Chamberlain, John. *The Enterprising Americans: A Business History of the United States.* New York: Harper & Row, 1963.

Dunbar, Seymour. *A History of Travel in America.* New York: Tudor Publishing Co., 1937.

Galloway, John Debo. *The First Transcontinental Railroad.* New York: Dorset Press, 1989.

Garraty, John A. *The American Nation: A History of the United States to 1877,* vol. 1, 5th ed. New York: Harper & Row, 1983.

Gies, Joseph, and Frances. *The Ingenious Yankees.* New York: Thomas Y. Crowell, 1976.

Groner, Alex. *American Business and Industry.* New York: American Heritage, 1972.

Heyn, Ernest V. *Fire of Genius: Inventors of the Past Century.* Garden City, N.Y.: Doubleday, 1976.

Holbrook, Stewart H. *The Story of American Railroads.* New York: American Legacy Press, 1947.

———. *The Yankee Exodus.* New York: Macmillan, 1950.

Hollingsworth, Brian. *The Illustrated Encyclopedia of the World's Steam Passenger Locomotives: A Technical Directory of Major International Express Train Engines from the 1820s to the Present Day.* New York: Crescent Books, 1962.

Hubbard, Freeman. *Encyclopedia of North American Railroading: 150 Years of Railroading in the United States and Canada.* New York: McGraw-Hill, 1981.

The Illustrated Encyclopedia of Science and Technology. New York: Exeter Books, 1979.

Jacobs, David, and Anthony E. Neville. *Bridges, Canals & Tunnels: The Engineering Conquest of America.* New York: American Heritage, 1968.

Jacobs, Timothy. *The History of the Pennsylvania Railroad.* Greenwich, Conn.: Bonanza, 1988.

Jensen, Oliver. *The American Heritage History of Railroads in America.* New York: American Heritage, 1975.

Klein, Aaron E. *The History of the New York Central System.* Greenwich, Conn.: Bonanza, 1985.

Langdon, William Chauncy. *Everyday Things in American Life, 1776–1876.* New York: Charles Scribner's Sons, 1941.

Lingeman, Richard. *Small Town America.* New York: G. P. Putnam's Sons, 1980.

Merk, Frederick. *History of the Westward Movement.* New York: Alfred A. Knopf, 1978.

Meyer, Balthasar Henry. *History of Transportation in the United States before 1860.* Washington, D.C.: Carnegie Institution, 1948.

Miller, Douglas T. *Then Was the Future: The North in the Age of Jackson, 1815–1860.* The Living History Library, John Anthony Scott, general editor. New York: Alfred A. Knopf, 1973.

Plowden, David. *Bridges: The Spans of North America.* New York: W. W. Norton & Co., 1974.

Shaughnessy, Jim. *Delaware & Hudson.* Berkeley, CA: Howell-North Books, 1967.

Schlesinger, Arthur M., Jr., ed. *The Almanac of American History.* New York: G. P. Putnam's Sons, 1983.

Smelser, Marshall, and Joan R. Gundersen. *American History at a Glance.* 4th ed. New York: Harper & Row, 1978.

Smith, Page. *The Shaping of America: A People's History of the Young Republic.* New York: McGraw-Hill, 1980.

Urdang, Laurence, ed. *The Timetables of American History.* New York: Simon & Schuster, 1981.

Williams, John Hoyt. *A Great and Shining Road: The Epic Story of the Transcontinental Railroad.* New York: Times Books, 1988.

Yenne, Bill. *The History of the Southern Pacific.* Greenwich, Conn.: Bonanza, 1985.

INDEX